Dedication

For my cutie pie, Ryan.
You have a fearlessness and passion about life
that most people will never know.
I am proud to be your father.

Contents

	Introduction	5
1.	The Story of Max	9
2.	Alphabet City	15
3.	Time Marches On	35
4.	Seeing Stars!	59
5.	The Chairperson Rules	69
6.	"Because I Don't Have To!"	81
7.	Teacher Training is Fundamental	91
8.	Advocating	113
9.	The Domino Effect	117
10.	Where Do We Go From Here	123
	Epilogue	125
	Acknowledgements	127
	Appendix	131
	Glossary of Terms	149

Introduction

I HAVE A LONG HISTORY OF FIGHTING with the North Shore School District, Long Island, New York since my son Max entered the Sea Cliff School for first grade.

What can be so important that I feel the need to fight with the very people entrusted with my son's education? The answer is very simple. My son Max is deaf; leaving him at the mercy of the cutthroat business known as Special Education. Special Education, a bureaucratic labyrinth filled with administrative egos, budgets, laws and regulations that parents must fight their way through in order to educate their child. Services are what parents seek creating an appropriate Individualized Education Plan (IEP) which becomes the prized possession. Services encompass a myriad of requests: special education classroom, reading services, math tutoring, extended school year, occupational therapy, speech therapy, counseling, audiology, etc. The list is as endless as it is exhaustive for parents fighting for these services to be placed on their child's IEP by reluctant school districts.

Max's first two years in District proved disastrous. Max was nine years old (entering third grade) barely reading at kindergarten level. This is the source of my particular fight with the North Shore School District as I sought necessary one-one-one reading services for Max that I believed would counter effect these two years and get him caught up to grade level. The District repeatedly refused the reading services by manipulating the special education process and laws opting instead to place Max in a situation where ineffective teachers further damaged his academic progress.

Any parent familiar with Special Education understands the irony involved in fighting the very people you wish to help but this is the only way. I fight because I want Max to learn.

I am not a lawyer, I am just a father.

I have spent years drilling people for information about special education law: attorneys, teachers, advocates, anybody and everybody whose ear I can catch. I fear I have become one of those people other people like to avoid. I am sure I've seen people turn and run as they see me coming down the street or in a store. I've searched the web until my eyes were bloodshot and the words became a blur. As the years drift by, I have become a minor expert in IDEA, No Child Left Behind and other laws associated with special education and civil rights for disabled children. I have become obsessed with winning services for my son and through the years I have been successful, lucky and defeated.

Today, at this moment, I am defeated. I have just lost my sixth Impartial Hearing with the District. When I appealed this decision to the New York State Review Officer, I lost again. But I am not finished fighting. Whenever I feel frustrated and overwhelmed by this situation, my mind instinctively drifts back to the same moment and suddenly it is eight years earlier and I am lying on the couch on a lazy Sunday morning. Max suddenly appears in front of me with his eyes glazed over ready to cry and says, "Daddy my ears don't work no more; I can't hear you."

Hearing impaired since two and half years old, Max was fitted with hearing aids and was developing like any child would and then suddenly during a typical Sunday morning cartoon fest he came up to me with hearing aids in hands and innocently announced they were broken. I remember there was no panic on my part, no effort to fix them as I knew deep in my gut, even as my mind and heart were not willing to accept it, that my son at three and half years of age made the unthinkable plunge in the world of deafness. I can only imagine what was going on in his mind as he looked at his father whose only expression could be one of heartbreak as he intuitively realized his daddy could not help him. Max then put his arms around my shoulders and began to comfort me.

And to this day, this is the image that keeps me fighting.

Before you read on though, this is not a gushy story of how a little boy overcomes his disability against all odds and becomes a great success with his father's help. That would be a great story but this isn't that story. Why not? Well….

First, Max is only twelve years old.

Second, I am not sure how helpful I am at this point.

This book is unapologetic as I name those whom I feel hurt my son: teachers, school administrators and state employees. I refuse to allow them to hide behind the thin veil of a bureaucracy claiming themselves victims, just cogs in a machine they cannot control. NO! You are not victims. Our children are the victims. My story is substantiated by Impartial Hearing testimonies, test results, audio tapes of CSE meetings, and written correspondence.

This is not by any means legal advice nor is it a how to book on Special Education.

This story can best be described as a twisted tale between a father and his son's school district and what I learned about dealing with nasty, cut-throat school administrators who stand in the way of a child's education.

1
The Story of Max

*"Today you are You, that is truer than true.
There is no one alive who is Youer than You."*
Dr. Seuss

When my son, Max went deaf at three-and-half years of age, I had no idea that I would spend most of my time fighting with a school district so my son could learn. But, as it turns out, this is precisely what I have been doing since we moved to the North Shore School District on Long Island, New York.

Max's diagnosis was like a sucker-punch to my heart; it was unexpected, quick and painful. One moment everything was fine and the next moment everything wasn't. The technical term the doctor used was enlarged vestibular aqueducts where the pressure damaged the membranes in the cochlea. But it didn't matter what the doctor called it. All that mattered was that Max wasn't hearing and it wasn't going to get better. Max had moderate to severe hearing loss in his left ear and severe to profound in his right. He told us the condition was irreversible and can graduate to total hearing loss. I wanted to curl up and grieve this news as only a parent with a hurt child could but there wasn't time. There were doctors' visits, hearing tests and decisions that needed to be made and I was afraid. It's bad enough when parents have a so called "perfect kid" that you worry you're going to screw up but now you have a kid with problems and the pressure just intensifies. Suddenly, you find yourself weeding through massive amounts of information, conflicting opinions from "experts" and well-meaning family members while trying to wrap your mind around the fact that your child has a disability.

My wife, Patrizia and I wanted to be prepared if Max lost his hearing completely, but there is no consensus on anything regarding the disability of deafness. A major decision was whether or not Max should get a cochlear implant if he went deaf. Means of communication for the hard of hearing and the deaf were plentiful but which are the right choices: auditory/oral only (no sign language), American Sign Language (ASL) only, total communication (auditory/oral and ASL), cued speech, and lip-reading. Questions regarding education were equally confusing; deaf schools vs. regular classrooms vs. blended classrooms vs. special education. The combinations seemed endless. There was no one clear-cut answer. Smacked with a bunch of opinions and personal choices; it made our decisions regarding Max more ominous.

It was during this time Patrizia and I decided to visit the John Tracy Clinic to better understand his disability. The John Tracy Clinic is a private, nonprofit education center for infants and preschool children with hearing loss in Los Angeles, California. The clinic offers free three-week summer programs to families who have children affected by hearing impairments and are an excellent resource for learning about "deafness" and all the variants involved from family life and education to the medical causes/implications. The clinic's expertise is spoken language development and learning through play and family routine.[1] This appealed very much to us as hearing parents of a child with a hearing disability. After our visit and much discussion, Patrizia and I decided that Max would be raised auditory/oral only and not learn sign language. We also decided Max would be fitted with a cochlear implant if he eventually lost his hearing completely. This meant that acquiring oral language skills would be the biggest hurdle Max would need to overcome; it would permeate every aspect of his life. Acquiring oral language skills is not easy for any deaf child but Max's experiences seemed more daunting since his descent into deafness was a graduated event that took place roughly over a 12-18 month period. Within this short timeframe, Max went from a hearing child, to a hearing impaired child to a deaf child and this process ultimately stifled the education process.

Initially, we had no idea anything was wrong with Max. He was taking longer to develop language skills but we rationalized it away as any parents in denial would. Don't boys develop more slowly than girls? It wasn't until the minimal words he acquired: daddy, mommy, cookie began to drop off that we sought medical help. He was two-and-half years of age but nobody knows the exact time Max began to lose his hearing. When I tell the story of Max; some people fail to understand why it took us so long to discover that our child wasn't hearing. Their frustration usually manifests into accusatory questions like, "How could you not know your son wasn't hearing?" or "Why didn't you take him to the doctors sooner?" I can appreciate their sentiments because I have asked these questions of myself a million times. But the reality is that sometimes it is not so easy to see that your child has a

---

1. http:www.jtc.org

problem; children are intelligent, crafty little creatures. And so discovering hearing loss in a child so young can be tricky since they learn to compensate quickly. Max would mimic us; he would laugh, smile, dance and cry all on cue creating the illusion that he was hearing.

When Max was finally diagnosed; he was fitted with hearing aids and began the arduous process of adjusting to acquiring information in a completely different way. Max began working with a speech therapist twice a week and he seemed to be on track. His language was coming along slowly and everyday he progressed. We tried to live life in the present but the fact that Max could lose his hearing completely at anytime made it incredibility difficult. It hung like a dark cloud over Max making us push him to learn.

Our fears came true a little less than a year later when Max came up to me and announced, "My ears are broken." Max lost his hearing completely, forcing him into a silent world for nine weeks while he waited for the cochlear implant surgery. During this time, we had very little communication with our son leaving him frustrated and confused. We were told to interact with him as usual but it was a particularly rough period for the whole family. Ryan, Max's older sister, was seven years old and didn't truly understand the significance of the situation and was left fending off her little brother who quickly developed the habit of hitting and grabbing to get attention. We felt helpless. Max was very aware of what he was missing and there wasn't a damn thing we could do about it.

Max had the cochlear implant surgery on his left side. The surgery took about four-and-half hours but it felt like a lifetime waiting for the surgeon to let us know if he was okay. Thankfully, Max made it through the surgery without incident but this was only the beginning. Max would need to go through the healing process, mapping of the implant (programming sounds) and months of rehabilitation. Even if the surgery was successful, the cochlear implant wasn't a magical cure; Max would again have to learn to process information in a different way and it could take weeks or months before he would be able to "hear" via the implant. As we planned for the unknown, wondering when Max would reap the benefits of the cochlear implant, Max surprised all of us. Four days after the cochlear implant was turned on, we observed the speech therapist working with Max, and watched as our son heard his first words, "up" and "down."

Max took to the implant like a fish to water but it couldn't undo damage caused by loss of time. His long drawn-out descent into deafness resulted in his gaining and losing information with repeated setbacks in speech and language development. He was almost four years old but essentially starting from scratch in his "hearing years" which regressed back to the infancy stage.

2
Alphabet City

"Treat people as if they were what they ought to be and you help them become what they are capable of becoming."
-- Goethe

WHILE AT THE JOHN TRACY CLINIC, I had heard stories from other parents who complained about not being able to get services for their child and I half heartedly listened. These parents threw around words like "appropriate" and "advocate" and were just angry at their kids' schools. I dismissed their tales of woe and thought quietly to myself, "Why don't they just move to a better school district?" The clinic even offered seminars in advocating for special education services which I foolishly dismissed. I remember I thought smugly, we live on the North Shore of Long Island with the best schools so this is never going to be a problem for us. I was cocky and sure I would not experience any problems and that my son would just go to school, get the services he needed and learn.

Then a little something I like to refer to as the BOCES bus incident occurred. BOCES are the Boards of Cooperative Educational Services in New York State that provide shared educational programs and services to school districts within the state.[2] The BOCES bus incident was

---
2. www.boces.org

my introduction to the bureaucracy that plagues public schools and it was a reality in which I was ill prepared. My expensive zip code offered no immunity.

Max was three-and-half years of age when he was enrolled in the Early Intervention Program at BOCES, Nassau County. Every day the bus took him to and from school and everything seemed to be going fine until one afternoon a few weeks into the year. Patrizia got a call from a friend who had a child in Max's class. She was calling because she wanted to know how Max was feeling since he wasn't in school. Patrizia called me at work hysterical and explained that Max wasn't in school today. Patrizia told me "Yes, Max got off the bus this afternoon like every other day," so the mystery of where Max was between getting on and off the bus had me imaging all kinds of horrific things. I didn't want to panic Patrizia more than she already was so I assured her that there must be a reasonable explanation. I told her I would follow the bus the next morning and find out what was happening. It was an incredibly long, sleepless night as I waited to find out what was happening to Max. The next morning finally arrived and we carried on with our usual routine with one small caveat. After Max was placed on the bus, I got into my car and followed. I parked across the street as the bus pulled up to the school. I sat and watched as all the school buses lined up. What I don't see are the children getting off the buses; this struck me as odd but I remained in my car. I waited some more and still nothing was happening. Finally, almost thirty minutes later staff members streamed out of the building and began to off-load the children. The mystery was solved.

Max got on the bus at 7:30 a.m.; the bus arrived at the school at 7:57 a.m., staff members started to off-load the children at 8:25 a.m., Max finally got off his bus at 8:55

a.m. The school day officially started at 8:30 a.m. Obviously, when Patrizia's friend dropped off her child, she didn't see Max because he was a half-hour late for school.

At this point I was more curious than upset and set up a meeting with the school principal to find out why this was happening and how often. During the meeting the principal explained that the staff was under contract to start at 8:25 a.m. which told me that Max and all these other children were just sitting on a bus everyday waiting to be off-loaded while the staff was inside doing nothing. Not only were the children late for school but they were being exposed to toxic fumes on a daily basis as the buses sat idle with the heat on due to the cold weather. Now, I was upset. The principal explained the situation as if it was acceptable to imprison 255 pre-schoolers on buses everyday because a "contract" was involved. After about a half an hour of going back and forth with her I gave up. It was clear she intended to do nothing for these children and I found her blasé attitude appalling. For the principal it was a simple black and white issue of a teacher contract and this contract clearly overrode any moral compass she may have had to find a safe solution for our children.

I immediately informed other parents about what was happening to our children. Some parents were equally outraged and others wanted us to leave it alone and not rock the boat. The idea of Max breathing in toxic fumes was criminal in my mind. I took exception to my son being put in an unsafe position and missing thirty minutes of school each day. Max's education was of the upmost importance to me, I wasn't looking for a babysitting service. As the weeks passed the issue really heated up but no resolution was in sight. During this time period, Patrizia and I were driving Max to and from school.

Then one family got Senator Hilary Clinton's office involved and an investigation into the whole program began. Months passed as the investigator(s) looked into the BOCES program and then finally there was an unintentional outcome. It turned out the bus issue ended up being the least of the principal's problems. Ultimately, the investigation yielded that the program was in violation of not having enough teachers-to-student ratio.

What amazed me was that the Principal was unwilling to work with us parents because of a "legal contract" with the teachers and yet had no trouble disregarding New York State Education Law as it relates to teacher-student ratio.

This incident, as grotesque as it was, taught me a valuable lesson that I would have to be vigilant for Max and not assume "all is well." Clearly, from an administrative point of view there were bigger issues at stake. Contracts and budgets took precedence while our children's well being and learning came in at a distant second. This realization fueled a desire in me to make sure my son's rights are always protected.

Patrizia kept in touch with staff members from the John Tracy Clinic and informed them that Max did indeed lose his hearing and had surgery for the cochlear implant. To our astonishment, they invited us back a second time because Max's case was unusual. Max would be facing new challenges now that he was deaf and had the implant and the clinic wanted to offer us a second chance to learn about things that weren't relevant our first visit. Naturally, we jumped at the opportunity. Keeping the BOCES bus incident in mind, I wasn't so smug and took this second opportunity at the clinic to take the seminars on advocating much more seriously. I listened to what parents were saying about their school districts and how their children were being denied needed services. I knew that I would have to advocate for Max despite fancy addresses and high ranking districts.

Given the events of last year, Patrizia and I were uncomfortable sending Max to another BOCES program and decided to put Max in a private nursery school at our own cost. During this time, we were living in Manhasset, N.Y. working with this school district and had few issues regarding Max's IEP. Our disagreements ranged from how many times a week Max should get speech therapy to when Max should start a particular program. When we told them we wanted Max to attend a private nursery school they didn't put up a fight, but then again, they weren't paying. Later, when we told them we wanted Max to attend Mill Neck Manor, a deaf school in Mill Neck, NY for kindergarten Manhasset agreed it was an appropriate placement and placed it on his Individualized Education Plan (IEP). Mill Neck Manor is a 4201 New York State approved school so New York State covers the cost versus school districts. Overall, our experiences with the Manhasset School District weren't horrible and they certainly weren't indicative of what was coming.

Max spent two years at Mill Neck Manor working with a wonderful teacher, Ms. Dawson who understood that Max's hearing age and language skills were stunted due to his particular situation. Max entered Mill Neck Manor at the chronological age of five with the hearing age of a one-and-a-half year old.[3] She worked well with Max developing his language skills and he enjoyed being in her class. Ms. Dawson also worked well with parents, a skill I would later find an anomaly in the field of

---

3. Using Normal Developmental Milestones with Very Young Children who have Cochlear Implants, Krista S. Heavner, MS CCC-SLP/LSLS Cert AVT.

Special Education. She took our concerns to heart and was never dismissive if we suggested something regarding Max's education.

Unfortunately, Max could not continue at Mill Neck Manor since the auditory oral program offered ended at the first grade. The other programs Mill Neck Manor offered stressed total communication and we were raising Max auditory/oral so we needed to find him a new placement for the fall. Two important criteria for Max's next school would be, one, that they work well with deaf students who had cochlear implants and two, had a reputation for being generous with services. Was I asking too much?

When I initially heard about the schools within the North Shore School District I thought I hit the Special Education lottery. I was in contact with a parent who had two children with cochlear implants in the North Shore School District and we had several discussions regarding the District and the services provided; never was a bad word uttered. Also, our daughter's teacher from Manhasset lived in the North Shore School District; had her daughter enrolled and also spoke highly of it. Everybody we spoke to on the subject kept saying it is the best District so we felt our due diligence was complete. Assured repeatedly the North Shore School District worked successfully with deaf children I confidently moved Max into District unwittingly placing him as a victim in an administrative game of hit and run. All problems prior to Max entering this District will pale in comparison. It wasn't until a few years later in the middle of my fight with the District that I discovered that the parent I was in contact with who had the kids with the implants had exaggerated her children's success for reasons I am still unsure… was it parental pride, fear or good old fashion denial? I will never know. They have since moved out of state. All I do know is that the end result of Max's first two years at the Sea Cliff School was an eight-year-old child reading well below kindergarten level and a father who was on the verge of a total meltdown.

But, I should have seen the trouble coming. The minute we decided to sell our house in Manhasset to move to the North Shore School District, my wife announced, "We should find separate places." If that wasn't a bad omen I don't know what is. I knew we were having problems but I wasn't prepared to end the marriage and was shocked she was. But money problems and just plain living had taken its toll so if she wanted out; I wasn't going to fight her. We agreed to find separate places in the District and share custody of the kids. Ryan was nine and Max was five when we told them we wouldn't be living together as a family anymore.

Of course, on the onset, things with the District seemed promising and I was excited for Max to be in one of the best school districts. What parents don't want the best for their child? Max was aging out of the Mill Neck Manor program and it was time for North Shore School District to live up to its reputation. It was now their responsibility to find an appropriate placement for Max. So the powers that be at the North Shore School District visited Mill Neck Manor to discuss Max's academic standing and a Committee on Special Education (CSE) meeting was to follow. Since Mill Neck Manor focused on language skills, Max still had not mastered the alphabet and didn't know the sounds of the letters but the District seemed confident they could teach Max.

Then another bad sign left me with an unsettling feeling. Just before the CSE meeting was to take place, I needed to drop off some paperwork at the school. While there I noticed that the Assistant Director of Special Education, Tom Korb was in his office and I thought it would be a good opportunity to introduce myself as a parent of a new kid coming into the District and have a friendly chat. Not to downplay any child's problem but the fact that deafness is not a common disability, I was worried about Max entering the District and was looking for a little reassurance. When I introduced myself and mentioned that Max is deaf as a means to distinguish which parent I was, his only response was, "We educate all kids here." When I attempted to explain that I know but Max's situation is different due to his graduated hearing loss, he stated again, "We educate all kids here." He repeated this canned response three times and I quickly surmised I wasn't going to get anywhere with this particular individual and left. Quite frankly, my encounter with Mr. Korb left me with an icky feeling and I was glad to be out of his presence.

I put these feelings aside because I felt I had an ace in the hole. Mill Neck Manor had instituted a courtesy program where the teachers helped their students mainstream into the public school system. Knowing Max would still be in contact with his previous teacher, Ms. Dawson and she would help the District transition him to his new learning environment was a comforting thought.

The day of the CSE finally arrived and I am a little anxious. I've attended CSE meetings before but still couldn't shake the overall oppressiveness of the situation. It is an odd feeling knowing you are about to walk into a room full of strangers about to dissect your child. Immediately, I am struck by a wall of people: Barbara Cooper, the Head of the Special Education Department, Tom Korb, Beth Lawatsch, special ed. teacher, Karen Demeo, the speech pathologist, a parent member and some others whom I can't recall. Talk about a home field advantage! Although the meeting began friendly enough; it was definitely an intimidating situation. The consensus was that Max should repeat the first grade at Sea Cliff School in an effort to help him catch up. Although, I wasn't crazy about the idea of Max repeating a grade, I agreed it was the right thing since he was so far behind. It was also decided that Max was going to be placed in a blended classroom (regular kids and special education kids) and receive additional support services such as speech and audio therapy, a teacher of the deaf, etc. The meeting was going fine and I was pleased with the services and the decisions overall. I mentioned Mill Neck Manor's program and Ms. Dawson's role in the transition thinking the school would welcome this idea. I couldn't have been more wrong. As the words left my mouth, the shift in the room from amicable to hostile was palpable as the District immediately went on the defensive rejecting Ms. Dawson's help. Personnel systematically began to list their qualifications and told us they didn't need a consultant. They each assured us they were perfectly capable of educating Max without outside help. Needless to say, I was not expecting the District to say, "No." I was stunned by their response and not prepared to counter their arguments. Who turns down free help? When I attempted to explain why I felt this was a good idea for Max and I wasn't questioning their abilities; they continued to balk and then Ms. Cooper abruptly ended the discussion announcing that it was against union contracts to have outside people observe their teachers. I couldn't understand their response, Ms. Dawson an experienced educator of the deaf was offering her services free as a courtesy to help a little boy and the District refused. The District's unwillingness to accept help from someone familiar with Max was a huge red flag.

I reluctantly acquiesced and let the District handle things

their way but I soon realized I made a big mistake. It didn't take me long to figure out that Max wasn't making any progress so Patrizia and I went up to the school to discuss our concerns. We were told to be patient; there was a learning curve for the relationship between teacher and student. When more time passed and Max was still not making progress, we went to the school again and were once again told to be patient. Finally after several weeks my patience was at an end. Personnel must have sensed my growing frustration and relented agreeing to let Ms. Dawson visit despite union contracts. But it ended up being a charade to appease me. Ms. Dawson told me that Karen Demeo refused to show her how she worked with Max during a speech session and Beth Lawatsch would not let her into the classroom. They only agreed to talk to her about Max's progress as a courtesy outside the classrooms. Turns out, Ms. Dawson was only allowed to evaluate Max in the lunch room which was pointless. Watching Max eat lunch was hardly going to give her any insight into Max's situation and why he wasn't making any progress. When Ms. Dawson finished with her "visit" she made us aware of the situation which I found unacceptable. I called the school in an attempt to work things out but it seemed an impossible situation. Ms. Cooper informed me that one of the teachers was filing a grievance against Ms. Dawson and she was not allowed on school property. Ms. Cooper would not tell me which teacher filed the grievance and never produced any paperwork. I couldn't believe this was the end result. The school's reaction seemed so over the top and not in line with Mill Neck Manor's experiences with other schools. Ms. Dawson mentioned that several students from Mill Neck Manor transitioned to public schools across Long Island and the program was welcomed in all of them except the North Shore School District.

It was early November and Max was losing valuable

education time. Max still didn't know the alphabet or the sounds of the letters and a new problem arose. He suddenly hated going to school which was never a problem in pre-school or Mill Neck Manor. Patrizia informed me that Max was crying and locking himself in the bathroom almost every day. I couldn't understand what was going on and why the change in his behavior.

Sea Cliff School invited parents for open houses several times a year to observe the kids and take part in school activities. During one of these open houses; I caught a glimpse of something and found my answer as to why Max suddenly hated going to school. The teacher had a projector and screen in the classroom showing slideshows of the kids in various situations. In all of them, kids were sitting together having fun, involved in some activity; painting, drawing, playing games and Max was on the outskirts alone. Max was always in the background away from the other children. He looked like a ghostly shadow hovering on the sidelines and in the background, otherworldly and removed. It was incredibly disheartening for me to see my son being treated this way.

Once I noticed the projector, I became hyper vigilant about what was going on and watched how everyone was treating Max. It was amazing how much I observed. Max was not interacting with the kids in his class and it didn't take me long to realize that he didn't even know their names. When I asked the Teacher of the Deaf why Max didn't know the names of the other children I was informed that he had a memory issue as though this made it all right. A Teacher of the Deaf is supposed to understand the issues related to educating deaf children and be able to help a child overcome such issues. Max needed to focus on one thing at a time before he could move onto the next but this is reflective of his being deaf and needing time to process information. If the Teacher of the Deaf didn't understand this basic criteria for teaching Max who else in the school would? A person certainly couldn't introduce him to a room full of kids and expect him to remember their names without a little effort. Max entered Sea Cliff School with minimal oral language skills and the hearing age of a toddler; this seemed to escape her attention making me question her abilities. I went around the room holding Max's hand introducing him to the kids. I asked Max which kids he liked and he pointed to the boys so I focused on them. I said each kid's name to Max several times and had him repeat the name back to me several times while the Teacher of the Deaf watched. Afterwards, I suggested that she focus on the boys Max liked and she told me she couldn't do that, it wasn't right. Was this practice of political correctness really necessary in first grade? This was a major issue and it had a rippling effect. As a consequence she failed to fulfill another important function which was to teach other people how to interact with Max and vice versa. So, not only wasn't Max learning but he had no friends and was ostracized from the class.

Most deaf children have a problem with working memory. Working memory is the ability to actively hold information in the mind needed to do complex tasks such as reasoning, comprehension and learning. Max had to work to hear the information and then had to concentrate to process the information and he had very little language skills to aid him. In simple terms, if a person was to ask Max to repeat, "One, two, three, four, five." Max would be so busy trying to process the words, one and two that three, four and five would get lost. Yes, Max had a memory issue related to his disability but this wasn't a new development in deaf education so why wasn't the District working on the issue instead of using it as an excuse. Memory is a hurdle but certainly not indicative of the intellectual capabilities of deaf children. The teachers should have been working with Max to develop his memory skills (i.e.: memory games, sequencing activities, rhyming activities, etc.) as part of his education.

I requested a CSE meeting to discuss my concerns that Max was not making any progress academically or socially. During this meeting, the educators proceeded to expound a litany of excuses:

• Mill Neck Manor exaggerated Max's level.

• The teachers were still getting to know Max.

• Max doesn't want to do the work.

• Max has a memory issue and cannot retain information.

• Max has a learning disability.

In short, none of it was their fault. I repeated my desire to have Ms. Dawson come in as a consultant but was rebuked yet again. I then offered to accept any consultant who had experience with the deaf to come in and work with the school but they would not budge on the issue at all.

Once again, I attempted to explain Max's background and how his situation was different from the other kids who had implants thinking maybe this was the source of the problem. The other children were born deaf and received the implants much earlier; Max got his at three-and-half years old so his "hearing age" was not on par with the other implanted kids. His language skills were not at their level. Yes, Max was seven years old but his hearing age was that of a three and half year old. They dismissed my explanation as though it were the rantings of a madman and not a legitimate factor in teaching Max. They kept rattling off their academic resumes instead of listening and they refused to accept any advice. I was completely frustrated and finally just came out and asked, "Do you believe you can give Max Gibson an appropriate education at Sea Cliff Elementary School?" Barbara Cooper replied "Yes!" The District held firm in their belief and now I had a child who in addition to not knowing the alphabet and sounds of the letters was regressing socially.

At this point, I didn't care who was to blame, I just wanted to know what the District was going to do to fix the problem. *What is the plan!* Either come up with a plan or admit you don't know what you're doing, but stop blaming everybody else, and take some responsibility. I told them I was filing for an Impartial Hearing seeking an outside consultant. I was promptly informed by Ms. Cooper that it was my right to do so. Her tone was dismissive and curt. It was reminiscent of the blasé attitude of the principal at BOCES and I walked out of the meeting shaken; worried I just placed my son in a very bad situation.

I couldn't afford private school and I didn't have the money to just pick up and move to another school district and even if I did, would I make it worse or better. (And yes, I see the irony of the situation, my harsh judgment of those parents at the John Tracy Clinic came back to haunt me again). I felt ineffective and bullied and taken advantage of by the people with whom I entrusted my son's education. Special Education Lawyers in New York are expensive so this really wasn't an option.

If I could afford to spend $350.00 an hour on an attorney and shell out $7,500.00 for a retainer I wouldn't be in this mess. It was up to me to advocate for my son and get him what he needed and this is not going to be an easy task. Despite the advocating seminars at the John Tracy Clinic, I was in over my head so I contacted an advocacy group on Long Island. The advocacy group guided me with information, useful websites and advice but the truth is, they are stretched beyond their resources and weren't telling me anything new. The philosophy of both the clinic and the advocacy group seemed to be in alignment. Basically a parent should work with the school district, present facts for their argument, compromise and above all else, don't make an enemy of the school district. But the classes cannot prepare parents for a wall of administrators and teachers that have one mind set. I did the best I could and familiarized myself with IDEA and No Child Left Behind and the process in general but it was incredibly overwhelming.

Shortly after filing for the Impartial Hearing, I received a call from Mr. Korb stating that they were going to add an outside consultant of their choosing to the IEP. I still have no idea what changed their mind. I was relieved for two very distinct reasons. I would not have to go through with the Impartial Hearing which absolutely terrified me and the consultant would be added to the IEP which offered me some relief that somebody would be evaluating what these teachers were doing with my son all day.

Although, I was finally able to get Max an outside consultant at what cost? Max's education suffered for months and the District would not utilize Mill Neck Manor's free services opting to pay for a consultant. They seemed hell bent on doing things their way even if it didn't make any sense to me. I believed the whole thing was a waste: a waste for Max, a waste of time for everyone involved and a waste of money when the services of Mill Neck Manor came free!

It is indeed a pennywise pound foolish system and after years of fighting in it this is what I learned. Nothing in life can prepare you for dealing with Special Education. Dante traveling through the circles of hell has nothing on me as I deal with the flurry of "red tape" and lies casually thrown at me by school administrators, teachers, psychologists and lawyers as I attempt to navigate my way through the murky waters of special education law trying to get services for Max.

Nothing is what it seems and to be effective, a parent needs to understand the realities of the situation versus the Pollyanna notions of special education that school district's want parents to believe:

- First, blind trust is the worst thing a parent can have when it comes to educating any child.

- Second, there is nothing really special about "special education." The word special implies unique, distinct, or unusual and this is just not the case. These children are very much at the mercy of whatever programs their school district offers negating anything "special."

- Third, school districts have a budget! Meaning, it's a business like any other so keep this in mind at all times. A budget means they will scrimp where they feel it is necessary so higher-ups will benefit and pensions will be funded. Children are a necessary evil they endure to keep their pockets lined. School administrators love the federal funds for special education rolling in the door but that doesn't mean children are going to get what they need.

- Fourth, teachers and administrators are only human. Just because they have masters degrees and certificates in special education doesn't mean they know anything about educating a child.

So if your child is diagnosed with a learning disability, a physical disability or mental disability whatever the case maybe it is now your job as a parent to help this child become as independent as possible which means this child needs to go to school. So for better or worse you need to prepare yourself for dealing with Special Education. This means Sorry Charlie; looks like you're going back to school to learn the ABC's of Special Education where the onslaught of information is like an assault on your mind. From the start, school districts have an edge. You've just been thrown into a game they have been playing for years. Suddenly, people start tossing a bunch of acronyms at you: CSE, IEP, FAPE leaving your head throbbing. You're stuck playing catch-up in a game that started way before you were even on the field. Then you find yourself sitting in meetings with "experts" talking above your head about your kid. And the end result is, when it comes to special education, the only one who isn't an expert on what your kid needs is you.

> **Now**......You need to attend a CSE to discuss an IEP where the goal is FAPE and don't worry cause we have an IDEA!

ABC's of Special Education
Pollyanna Crap vs. Reality

CSE Meeting (Committee on Special Education): a meeting where your child's IEP (Individualized Education Plan) is discussed. The CSE Meeting is a collaboration between parents and school personnel to discuss the goals, methods and services the school will utilize to teach your child.

CSE Meeting (Committee on Sub-Standard Expectations): a meeting where school personnel pigeonholes your child's potential keeping goals low to show a false positive on your child's progress thereby keeping the need for services at a minimum.

IEP (Individualized Education Plan): describes the goals and objectives set for a child during the school year, as well as any special support needed to help achieve them.

IEP (Inclusive Education Plan): details the substandard goals and objectives along with the services the school will supply. And coincidently it just so happens they have the exact services your kid needs on site.

IDEA (Individual Disability Education Act): law which governs special education and protects the rights of children with disabilities.

IDEA (Ill-defined Disability Education Act): law that allows school districts to hide behind subjective wording such as appropriate and reasonably calculated.

3
Time Marches On

"Lost time is never found again."
Benjamin Franklin

THE THING I FIND MOST HORRIFYING is the loss of time… tick, tock, tick, tock, and another day is gone. Can't get it back, gotta move forward. One more day gone by that my kid isn't getting what he needs. Time just goes about its business, marching on relentlessly, while I fumble through CSE meetings, and Impartial Hearings. Meanwhile, Max is getting older and windows of learning opportunities are closing forever.

The Internet was my ally and I obsessively researched anything and everything related to deafness. However, the only real conclusion I could draw from all this research was that the Internet is full of information that can scare the hell out of you. Although, I read a tremendous amount of information regarding deafness and literacy there were two facts that terrified me.

- Deaf children as the norm graduate from high school with a 4th grade reading level.[4]

---

4. Gallaudet Research Institute. 1996. Stanford Achievement Test, 9th Edition, Form S, Norms Booklet for Deaf and Hard-of-Hearing Students. (Including Conversions of Raw Score to Scaled Score & Grade Equivalent and Age-based Percentile Ranks for Deaf and Hard-of-Hearing Students.) Washington, DC: Gallaudet University.

- Two-thirds of students who cannot read proficiently by the end of the 4th grade will end up in jail or on welfare. The fourth grade is the watershed year.[5]

It was obvious to me that no matter what decision a parent made with respect to deaf or hearing impaired children: cochlear implants, ASL, auditory/oral, total communication, etc., there is a massive stumbling block in the education of deaf children and this has nothing do with a deaf child's ability to learn. From my point of view, this made deafness an underdog in the world of education. Although, the challenge of deafness has been around forever there have been no great strides in teaching literacy to the deaf. My only reasoning was that deafness didn't offer the same cache as other disabilities. Yes, research had been done to try and pin point the problem in teaching literacy to deaf children but the fact remains that it is a low incident disability and there has been no National Call to Arms to get these children reading. It has never received the recognition as the more recently diagnosed learning disabilities or the momentum that autism has recently sparked in the education world. Deafness has never been glamorized as a cause célèbre; there have been no massive campaigns by parents for a better understanding of deaf education. Max has an obscure disability that had eluded the education world and now I had to deal with this very real issue. Max's future was contingent on finding a way to educate him and the first year in Sea Cliff School proved this wasn't going to be an easy task. My fears for Max were now a reality. Max was well on his way to becoming a part of the statistical "norm" for deaf students and I wasn't going to let this happen to my son.

Time is a special education parent's worst enemy.

---

5. National Assessment of Adult Literacy (NAAL), Literary Statistics

3: Time Marches On

Even when the system is working perfectly, it is a grueling time-stealing process essentially set up to move the child along so that by the time a parent not happy with their child's IEP is done attending CSE meetings, filing paperwork, attending Mediations, Resolution meetings and Impartial Hearings, the school year has come and gone without the services.

There are very few options for parents frustrated with their child's IEP.

- Parents can pull their child out of the system and pay for private school.

- Parents can keep their child in the district but pay for additional services themselves.

- Parents can choose the options listed above and seek their money back on the backend through an Impartial Hearing or court hearing which is a huge gamble.

- Parents can move into another school district acquiring a whole new set of problems, another big gamble.

- Parents can stay in their current district and continue to fight for services.

But it is more than just the system itself that holds our children back. School Districts take advantage of this process and stretch it out longer than necessary ensuring that services are pushed off. Since most parents fall into the latter category of staying in district, the combination of the process and a school district's resistance ensures that children lose. Let's face it, if parents could afford private school for their kids, suddenly the special education administrators in the public school system would be singing a different tune because they would be out of a job. The reality is that parents are stuck and the administration knows we are stuck.

Time is a major tactical advantage for school districts keeping parents in a perpetual state of stuckness. Time is a luxury that school districts possess that children simply do not have. Parents need to understand how a school district will waste time to rob a child of education. Indeed, school districts have so mastered the art of procrastination that any student would be envious of their superior techniques:

- ***Wait and see approach.*** This is when the educators know their approach or methods of teaching are not working but want parents to give it some time and see where it goes anyway. I feel this approach describes Max's first two years at Sea Cliff School. Who decides how much time should go by before the waiting stops and the action starts? Children should not have to suffer through days, weeks, months, or years of frustration caused by ineffective methods and poorly trained teachers.

- ***We don't have an appropriate placement yet but sit tight and we'll figure something out plan.*** One minute they are sitting in CSE meetings telling parents they know how to educate a child then suddenly when they realize they cannot educate the child, these same people want to delay the process because they need to figure out things out. Suddenly, the education experts morph into fumbling bureaucrats and it's amateur hour while they look into options, investigate schools, speak to various people, wait for someone to get back to them, have a call out, need to put a call in, need to request board approval and need to wait on the board approval. Most programs and schools have been around long enough and chances are the School District has already dealt with a parent in the past requesting the same service.

- ***Scheduling Conflicts:*** due to M.I.A. personnel for various reasons: vacation, jury duty, sick, hang nail. School Districts know weeks even months in advance which personnel are going to be needed at any given CSE meeting or Impartial Hearing. A child's education shouldn't be put on hold because adults cannot get their scheduling right. School Personnel should treat CSE meetings and Impartial Hearings with the significance they deserve.

- ***Incomplete IEP:*** Goals aren't finished; computers are down…basically anything and everything to delay a Free Appropriate Public Education (FAPE) causing the need to reschedule CSE meetings.

- ***Getting to Know A Child:*** It shouldn't take a teacher six months to familiarize themselves with a child to the point where it affects the education process.

- ***Lost Invitations:*** The school district forgets to invite necessary personnel to the CSE meeting causing the meeting to be rescheduled.

When a parent finally gets sick of the *wait-and-see approach* and no longer trusts their School District to *figure things out*, things can go south pretty fast. At this point, School Districts start to pull other delaying tactics and suddenly everything comes to a screeching halt. School Districts understand the importance of time in these matters so they turn the screws – just get this kid through another day, another week, another month, another year without providing services. The very thing a parent is trying to avoid is the very thing a School District is capitalizing on because it's just another day they don't have to pay!

The North Shore School District has delayed or elongated CSE meetings and Impartial Hearings with a plethora of excuses:

- On several occasions the school psychologist was out of town.

- We couldn't finish a CSE meeting because the goals were not correct so we had to reschedule another meeting, 24 days later.

- An Impartial Hearing was delayed because a major witness, Max's reading teacher was on jury duty. This Impartial Hearing dragged on three months, October thru December 2008.

- Scheduling conflicts with the District were a constant struggle.

- District claimed that they didn't get the request for a CSE meeting.

- CSE meeting in April 2010 dragged on for three hours only to find out the goals were not ready, due to a computer glitch and the meeting would have to be rescheduled.

- CSE meeting dated May 2010, (rescheduled from April 1 2010), Marcy Laredo, Assistant Special Ed. Director, dragged out the meeting by talking for two hours about what happened at the previous CSE meeting.

My opinion is that school districts use these "delay tactics" to accomplish very specific goals:

- Anger

- Confusion

- Frustration

- Exhaustion

They want parents angry, confused, and tired because they are a less viable opponent. A parent cannot make a "reasonable" argument if they fall prey to these tactics. They also count on these tactics to dissuade parents from coming back. Make it impossible for you to fight: time off work, time away from your other children and time away from spouse. These little games can cost parents dearly: jobs, time, energy, money, relationships. The occasional snafu is understandable but when it occurs repeatedly, the school is definitely practicing a defensive stance of delay, delay, delay.

Another, tactic I was recently introduced to is something called the Delphi Technique, an unethical means of getting consensus from a group. It is basically a divide and conquer technique whereby the facilitator of the meeting finds out where the other attendees stand on a subject. Once the facilitator has this knowledge, they can manipulate this information to their predisposed outcome. When an opponent of their opinion asks a question, the facilitator avoids the questions or doesn't really answer the question asked. Another major part of the technique is making their opponent agitated so they appear irrational while the facilitator remains calm and rational.[6] After reading about this technique I began to

---

6. www.iror.com

wonder if this in fact was being used by the chairpersons at CSE meetings for Max. Of course, I have no proof but looking back through the years I've experience all aspects of the Delphi Technique: polling, avoidance of questions and answers not related to questions.

All these tactics are incredibly difficult to overcome. There is no system set in place to prevent the schools from taking advantage of time or utilizing an unethical tactic to create consensus.

Regrettably, I will spend another year attempting to work with the North Shore School District letting promises made by personnel override my gut instincts. It was almost the end of Max's first year at Sea Cliff when I received a call from the school. I was in the middle of a business meeting but recognized the number so I stepped out of the room and picked up to hear Dr. Perez, the school psychologist's voice on the other side. The conversation started with the usual pleasantries but I felt he wanted to tell me something but was having a hard time finding the words. He seemed hesitant but finally managed to get to the point, apparently, Max said something upsetting that concerned them. I couldn't imagine what Max could say that would upset the "school" and I was more curious than anything else when Mr. Perez stated that Max said, "I don't want come here anymore nobody likes me. I have no friends." These words hit my heart hard and all I could think of was Max, this adorable seven year old boy always smiling, friendly, who in my eyes was being hurt by a school so ill prepared for his attendance that they created an outcast out of him. We agreed to meet immediately. Visibly shaken, I went back in the meeting to collect my things, made a quick apology to a confused room full of people and abruptly left. Walking to my car, my emotions teetered between anger at the school and sadness for my son who was so unhappy. His words "Nobody likes me. I have no friends" still ring in my ears and have the same effect, heartbreak.

I called Patrizia and made arrangements to meet her at the school. I was hoping, praying, one person in the room would state the truth of the matter; Max was not in the right placement. As I entered the meeting, I was still shaking. I felt all the months of stress of Max's first year coming to a head. I wanted to confront these people and get Max out from under them but I didn't know how. I wanted to lash out but knew that wouldn't serve Max, I had to sit and listen to what they were going to say. I expected the usual defensive statements so I was caught completely off guard when the Principal and teachers apologized. My anger quickly shifted to confusion. Everyone was being so nice and agreeable; all the tension from meetings past seemed to be gone. They expressed how upset they were and had no idea that Max was feeling so badly. Then they made promises that his next year at Sea Cliff would be different. I didn't believe them but didn't want to provoke an argument. Could they be so completely out of touch? How do they think a child would feel if they had no friends? It didn't make a difference. The only thing I wanted to hear from the school was that they were not able to educate Max but they obviously weren't ready to admit that just yet. After an entire year of the District playing the blame game my trust level was zero. And I had a more pressing problem on my mind. Forcing the teachers to work with a consultant via the threat of an Impartial Hearing could obviously create a lot of ill will. I was afraid the teachers would take their frustrations out on Max so I decided to play nice in a pre-emptive attempt to avoid problems for the upcoming school year.

3: Time Marches On

Max's second year at Sea Cliff started off optimistically. We were generally pleased with the IEP, and Max was working with a new reading teacher, Carol Speranza. I didn't like that he was still working with Karen Dameo, the speech therapist. I felt Ms. Dameo accomplished nothing with Max his first year and I didn't trust her to move past her feelings that she expressed so openly regarding Max and Mill Neck Manor. In spite of my reservations, Max enjoyed going to school again and he seemed to like his second grade teacher Ms. Roberts. With Max happy and no complaints from Patrizia, I assumed things at the school were moving along. I picked the kids up after school on Tuesdays and Thursdays and we followed a routine of going to the playground and getting pizza before heading home for homework.

There seemed to be a lull and I was actually able to relax. But eventually the truth revealed itself when I noticed Max was bringing home the same three reading books night after night. These books are about 8 – 10 pages long with approximately 18 different words in the book.

An example:

On the first page there was a picture with a frog on it. On the facing page the sentence read "The frog is on the rock." The next page had a turtle on it. On the facing page the sentence read "The turtle is on the rock" and so on and so on....

When I would ask Max to get his books so we could read them, he was doing the most peculiar thing. He raced to get the books from his book bag and ran back to me as I sat on the couch. He would bring two books at a time; one in each hand; then he would take the book in his right hand and hold it to the right side of head and recite the entire book and then take the book in his left hand and hold it to the left side of his head and recite this book to me. After Max completed this ritual, he would look at me and say, "Done!" He looked like a weird short version of the Amazing Kreskin's spewing off the contents of an object held to his head. I had to laugh; he looked so ridiculous. Then I became curious and started to test him. I would read random pages and try to trick him but he would wag his finger at me and make the necessary correction. Max knew automatically what came next, so not only did he know the books by heart; he also knew the exact order of the stories. Very quickly, it became the beginning of a not so funny problem. I wasn't laughing anymore.

When I would offer up different books to Max; he absolutely refused to look at them. It became a struggle just to get him to sit on the couch with me if he noticed a book other than the school's books in my hands. When I forced the situation, he would cry and carry on and run for his school books. The scene was unreal. I was furious; Max was obviously not reading but reciting these books from memory. The irony of the situation wasn't lost on me either; the educators at Sea Cliff insisted Max had a memory issue and yet he was reciting the contents of these books without so much as a breath between words.

If the books didn't represent a big enough problem, the word worksheets sent home were disasters. A simple worksheet connecting the words with the pictures nearly drove me to an early grave. I would point to the picture of a bird and ask Max for the word; he had no idea. I would write the alphabet on top of the worksheet to give him clues. "Bird starts with a "b" Max", and I would point to the "b" on top of the page and he was still clueless. I refused to give him the answers and made him work on it until it was complete. Sometimes it took hours; I would drop off the kids to their mother completely exhausted.

Another oddity was that Max was not bringing home spelling words to study or completed spelling tests. He was getting them in first grade but now nothing. I tested Max myself and it was clear he didn't know all of the letters of the alphabet. He could repeat a letter if it is said to him but couldn't identify a letter on a page. Max's language was coming along but the transition to understanding written letters and the understanding of what sounds letters made was eluding him.

Something was off. The teacher told me the primer books are used to develop reading skills and my reaction was, "What reading?" He didn't know the alphabet, he didn't know the sounds of the letters, and he had very little sight word recognition. Sight words are words recognized immediately by a reader and are critical in learning to read. **A, and, not, no, out, in, his, her, this, that** are all examples of the basic 220 sight words included in the Dolch sight word list. On average a child should be able to recognize all 220 sight words by the end of third grade.[7] I felt the teachers needed to refocus on the very basics; one thing at a time and build. Nobody was listening. They were coming at Max from every direction and it wasn't working.

I repeatedly try to discuss my concerns with Patrizia about the books and the spelling tests but she told me everything was fine and the conversation stalled. She still trusted the school and couldn't see where there was

---

7. Source: Dolch, E.W., Ph.D. (1948). *Problems in Reading*. Champain, IL: The Garrard Press.

3: Time Marches On

a problem. She told me to leave it alone, and "Why are you looking for trouble?" Max was now eight years old and still didn't know his ABC's and suddenly I felt like the bad guy because I wanted to help my son. Now, in addition to the school I had another problem with which to contend. This was the first time Patrizia and I didn't agree on a plan of action when it concerned Max and I was unsure of how to proceed. We were at a stand-off and Max was going to suffer.

Despite the outside consultant, it was evident within the first few months of the new school year that things had not improved. It was disheartening knowing my son was going to school every day and not making gains. During the parent/teacher conferences the teachers would say Max was progressing and showed us reports, for the life of me, it was like we were talking about two different kids. If Max was making progress I saw no evidence of it outside their reports. I had a sinking feeling that Carol Speranza and Karen Demeo were on a steady course with disaster and I couldn't stop it.

Always looming in the back of my mind was the dark statistic about children who don't learn to read by the 4th grade. I couldn't shut this thought off. When I vented my concerns to family and friends they would tell me to fight for services without Patrizia. Although they meant well, unless you are a parent dealing with Special Education, a person cannot understand everything that is involved. I told them this is impossible. It's hard enough to get services when both parents are fighting never mind parents who disagreed. Our disagreement gave the school the freedom to ride out the school year.

I pressed forward trying to teach Max myself which was a complete and utter fiasco. I tried to remember all the things taught to me at the John Tracy Clinic but I was not qualified to teach him. When he would come over, I would continually push him to sit with me and read books. He refused and it would turn into a fight. Ryan shied away in a corner or tried to "protect" her brother. It became a test of wills between us coming to a head when Patrizia called me one evening and told me "Ryan and Max don't want to come over any more. Ryan doesn't like the way you are always pushing Max and thinks you are being mean." Patrizia went on to say, "You are driving your children away." What was worse was I knew she was right. I could see they didn't want to come into the apartment and it broke my heart. I felt like I had no choice and immediately backed off. It was clear nothing was going to happen until Patrizia was back on board.

It was one of the hardest things I ever had to do in my life. Now, when I picked up the kids, it was nothing but fun, fun, fun. I felt like Ryan and Max would "tell on me" if I stepped out of line resulting in swift punishment. First the School District, then Patrizia and now the kids! They all had me cornered and now I had to play the affable idiot until God knows when.

Months went by but the day finally arrived; Patrizia called. By the sound of her voice she was obviously upset. She explained that Max wasn't reading and that I should, "Do something about it!" I finally had permission to help my son. I had to move fast, the end of the year was coming. My plan was to attend the annual CSE meeting for the following year and not leave the room until something was done to resolve the situation.

After two years in District; Max had made minimal gains. His tri-annual testing (which is required for kids with disabilities) was bleak. He made six months worth of progress in a 24 month period. This was unacceptable. Max was entering third grade in the fall but he was barely reading at a kindergarten level. During the course of these two years Patrizia and I attended three CSE meetings and several parent/teacher/administrative conferences regarding the ability of this school to educate Max. The educators always reassured us that everything was fine and that Max was progressing and showed us reports to back up their statements. In the first two CSE meetings, we were told the school could teach Max and it was the same response in every conference we attended on the subject. "We can teach Max, Max is progressing and we don't need a consultant." The District's resolve never wavered.

When we showed up for the annual CSE meeting in early May 2008 we were met with the newly promoted Director of Special Education, Tom Korb and the entourage that followed him into the room: Carol Speranza, Ms. Roberts, Karen DeMeo, etc. So far my dealings with Mr. Korb had been minimal but I couldn't imagine this was going to go well given my initial meeting with him two years ago. He was exactly as I recalled; very formal and detached in appearance and speech. Although, I was prepared for a fight to get the District to admit that it was not the right placement, my plan was thwarted by none other than the District itself. The District's tune had miraculously changed, after two years; Mr. Korb announced that they wanted to move Max to an out-of-district placement. I was relieved for about a nanosecond when Mr. Korb finished up by saying that they were investigating such placements for the fall school year. September was four months away. Mr. Korb was taking no immediate action choosing to let Max flounder for the remaining 20% of the school year and an entire summer until an out-of-district replacement could clean up their mess.

Then I had to continue to sit in this meeting while Mr. Korb's entourage backed his decision. Some personnel, Carol Speranza and Ms. Roberts didn't say anything but their silence by no means relieved them of their culpability in my mind. They could have intervened and stood up for Max. Karen DeMeo, on the other hand, was highly vocal. She seemed defensive and brought up Mill Neck Manor's evaluation of Max. Mill Neck Manor was two years ago and irrelevant in my opinion. Even if Max was not at the level Mill Neck Manor stated, there should have been more movement in Max's ability to understand the sounds of the letters. Personnel also re-iterated that Max had a learning disability and memory issues. This was not new information at this point. I felt like they were blaming a seven year old boy.

Two years of learning gone never to be recovered.... Tick, tock, tick, tock....The North Shore School District cost Max two years of learning. *Yes, Mr. Gibson we sat in meeting after meeting claiming to be able to educate your son and now we want to move him out-of-district without any repercussions.* They came to the table with nothing but excuses and wanted to neatly wash their hands of the whole matter. They no longer wanted "more time" and all the progress they claimed he was making suddenly diminished and now they wanted out.

When I stated that I felt the District should be doing something now to help Max, Mr. Korb managed a professional stance and repeated the special education mantra, "We are looking into things." This definitely falls under the category; ***we don't have an appropriate placement yet but sit tight and we will eventually fig-***

3: Time Marches On

ure it out. (In December 2008 I attended an Impartial Hearing as a direct result of these events, I heard Carol Speranza, Max's reading teacher testify that by the end of the first marking period, January 2008, four months into the school year she "had concerns about his functioning." Patrizia and I were never told of such concerns. The District waited three months, April 2008 for the CSE meeting to drop the news that it was time to move Max out of district and had no placement for him. There was no sense of urgency on their part and certainly no apologies for wasting Max's time. And make no mistake, it was Max's time).

The clock was ticking and I felt the walls closing in on me. Every time I wanted to make a move to help Max, it was like the special education process itself was pushing me back. Just requesting an outside consultant took months because it almost escalated to an Impartial Hearing. My only choice was to try and wade through it, hoping I would be able to help Max. By now I was infuriated and in a state of panic. In the back of my mind, all I could think of was Max and how much time he was losing while the District did nothing.

Even though the School District was satisfied with doing nothing, I wasn't going to sit idly by while our son lost more time. Patrizia found out about a place called Lindamood-Bell, a private reading program, located in our area that was successful in teaching reading to children with various learning difficulties. Since this was really the only option we had, we ran with it. I immediately set up an appointment with Carl Martin who is the Director of the Roslyn, NY location. I explained the situation and Mr. Martin said, "Nothing can be done without an evaluation of Max's abilities." He told me that Max would need to take a series of tests which usually last about 4 ½ hours." Then he directed me to reception to schedule the testing. The receptionist, Courtney suggested I bring Max in the following Wednesday and the evaluation will cost $425.00. The words were leaving her mouth and all I could think was another week, another week Max had to wait. She must have seen the look of utter desperation on my face and quickly said, "If you want, you could bring him in an hour." I told her I would be back as soon as I could. One problem solved; now, I had another. It is embarrassing to admit but I didn't have the money to get the tests done. Walking out of their office, I called my friend Scott and quickly explained the situation. His response was an immediate, "Cash or check?" I made all the necessary arrangements and went to the school to get Max. I ushered a confused Max into the car and quickly explained about Lindamood-Bell and the tests. He didn't fully understand what I was saying but he agreed he would try hard. After a quick introduction to Carl and Daryl, the Assistant Director of the clinic; Max was escorted off to begin the testing. I walked outside anxious and decided that I would distract myself by driving for the next few hours.

I got a call from Mr. Martin about an hour and half into the testing. He explained that Max wasn't able to complete some of the tests and confirmed Max's reading skills were barely at kindergarten level. Max was off the charts in some areas resulting in no score at all. The news was grim and incredibly difficult to hear but at least I had an accurate understanding of Max's ability. Mr. Martin explained that Max would need extensive one-on-one remedial reading tutoring, at least two hours a day for the remainder of the school year and twenty hours a week during the summer to begin the process of learning to read. When I pressed for a timeframe because I didn't want Max to spend weeks in a program with nothing to

3: Time Marches On

show for it Carl said, "It doesn't take weeks or months to know if a child is going to respond to a program. If Max doesn't show some improvement within a couple of days, we will change the program and try something else." He told me I was welcomed to come each week and watch the session and see how Max was progressing. Two years in District and nobody ever used the word "change" when it came to their method or approach or even hinted that something might not be working as a result of their efforts. I felt incredibly comfortable with Lindamood-Bell's philosophy of teaching. We had to take a chance that this would work for Max so the plan was to go back to the District and get them to place Lindamood-Bell on Max's IEP.

Lindamood-Bell is not a New York State approved school therefore school districts usually resist putting these types of programs on a child's IEP. The main reason is that school districts will have to pay versus the state. School districts do not like to pay for any service where the money is coming directly out of their pockets. Of course, school districts deny this ugly truth about special education and claim other reasons are the source of their decisions i.e.: IEP supplies FAPE without the service, but I think everybody knows the reality of the situation. Patrizia and I knew the odds but would not be deterred. We felt we had a good case and met with Mr. Korb to request Lindamood-Bell services for Max.

In a perfect world Mr. Korb's response would have been, "Yes, Mr. Gibson, we screwed over your son for the last two years and we will be happy to rectify the situation with reading services no matter what the cost." In reality, we got a bunch of stammering and excuses, "I don't know about the program, I will have to get back to you." When I asked what the District planned to do for Max. He countered, "We are waiting to hear back from the out-of-district schools." When I insisted that Lindamood-Bell be placed on the IEP, Mr. Korb ended the discussion with, "I cannot commit to these services." I walked out angry and planned to file for an Impartial Hearing. Tom Korb was stonewalling us. If he could push off reading services until the fall, he wouldn't have to pay for them. In the fall, the out-of-district placement would be supplying reading services and Mr. Korb would be off the hook. A few days later we got our official response and it was no surprise to me. He called and told me that he was informed by the District's attorney that Lindamood-Bell was not a New York State Approved Program and he could not place it on the IEP. He shot down our suggestion solely on its approval status but made no suggestion of his own to rectify the situation with Max. I felt like Tom Korb didn't care about Max.

I was no longer a novice special education parent and knew that the District had not supplied FAPE for the two years Max had languished at the Sea Cliff School suffering with their *wait-and-see-attitudes*. The District was not going to settle so easily this time and it looked like I was actually going to have to follow through with an Impartial Hearing. This thought scared me to death. I kept in contact with a woman, Valery from an advocacy group on Long Island who quickly walked me through the Impartial Hearing process. She told me that the School District would need to set up a Resolution meeting within 15 days of my filing. She advised me to try and work with the District and told me to settle if they came up with an offer. I attempted to follow her advice and went into the Resolution Meeting with an open mind. Once again, the District came to the table empty handed. The meeting was a waste of time so the

3: Time Marches On

next step was a Mediation Meeting. Once again I was told to follow the rules and go to Mediation to show that I was attempting to work with the School District.

Max's tri-annual testing and the scores from Lindamood-Bell were dismal and were proof enough that the District had failed him. But, things are not so simple when it comes to Special Education. IDEA is a highly subjective law and is set up for a parent's failure in fighting for services. After all, no school can guarantee that a child is going to learn. Deep down, the teachers and administrators in the District must have known they failed Max. I was having an incredibly hard time trying to understand why this District was not doing everything they could do to undo this wrong.

Then the morning of the Mediation Meeting; I unexpectedly got call from Tom Korb. He stated that the District wanted to offer a settlement agreement and that I should come to his office to go over the details of the agreement. I was floored but I wanted to keep the meeting on neutral territory and suggested we meet where the mediation was supposed to take place. He seemed annoyed that I was dragging him out of his office but relented. Driving over to Hempstead for the meeting, I was nervous and excited to review the agreement. I wasn't sure what to expect. The District was offering 220 hours at Lindamood-Bell to be utilized over the summer. I wasn't fool enough to think that 220 hours was enough to make up for two years but I figured it was a start. Then I read a stipulation in the agreement that made me incredibly uncomfortable. It stated that I legally gave up any rights to bring up these "two years" in any other future dealings with the District. The matter was essentially closed. I couldn't sign it. As much as I wanted those 220 hours I knew deep down it wasn't enough and that signing it was the same as letting these people off the hook. I walked out, praying I didn't make the biggest mistake of Max's life.

I would have to go through with the Impartial Hearing. Preparing witnesses and questions for a legal battle was not exactly how I pictured things going when I enrolled Max in school. The whole thing seemed so surreal; I couldn't believe it escalated to this level. To make matters worse, I didn't realize how long an Impartial Hearing could take when I turned down the settlement agreement. I was informed, it could take anywhere from three to six months and sometimes even longer. If the Hearing dragged on that long the entire summer would be over and the reason for starting this whole process would be moot but the damage had been done and now I had to move forward.

Walking into the preliminary for the Impartial Hearing was scary. This was the first time I was actually coming face to face with the District's attorney who by coincidence happened to have the same name, Gibson. Sharing a name with a person whose job is to help deny your child services is odd and off putting and then she began to speak rattling off the details of Max's history with proficient coldness and legal ease. One thought kept swimming through my head, "Why didn't I sign that settlement agreement?" As I fumbled with paperwork and struggled with legal procedures, the most wonderful thing happened. The Hearing Officer, Dr. Monk asked me a few questions and suddenly I was telling the story of Max and what happened over the last two years. When I told him that Mr. Korb told me the District couldn't place Lindamood-Bell on an IEP, he pointedly stated that I could readdress the issue at the hearing, "In the course of doing that, there is an opportunity again for

3: Time Marches On

you to suggest that, be it an approved or a non-approved program. An unapproved program can be taken into consideration but only for very specific reasons." I don't think that Attorney Gibson was happy about the turn the meeting was taking because she tried several times to interject during my exchange with Dr. Monk. I was clueless and didn't understand that Dr. Monk's reaction may have been a huge red flag for the District.

The second morning arrived and Dr. Monk asked "Is there is anything to be discussed before we continued with the hearing?" I responded "If we continue it will take the entire summer making the point of the hearing moot since the whole point is for Max to be receiving services during this time." At this point Attorney Gibson informed us that the District was ready to settle. I was overwhelmed by the whole experience, and the words, "Get something now and fight for more later," rattled in the back of my head. I was confused and paralyzed with fear; I couldn't afford to make a wrong decision. This time the District offered less than the previous settlement agreement and informed me it was due to administrative costs for going through with the Impartial Hearing. The stipulation from the original agreement was also included. The District's offer was a slap in the face for two lost years and they knew it. If I refused, the Impartial Hearing would continue and I could risk losing everything. Max would definitely lose the summer. If I agreed to the settlement Max would get something now and I could fight for more later. I felt like I was on some weird version of *Let's Make a Deal* but no matter what I chose Max was going to lose. The only question was by how much? Never before did I feel like I had a proverbial gun to my head.

I reluctantly signed the agreement.

4

Seeing Stars

*"Free the child's potential,
and you will transform him into the world."*
Maria Montessori (1870–1952)

WHEN WE FIRST WENT to the John Tracy Clinic, we were given a brief history of its origins. In 1924 Louise Tracy and her husband actor, Spencer Tracy, had a son John who was born with profound hearing loss. Frustrated by her inability to find information or guidance as to how to teach John and flanked by the medical opinion of her day [which equated deaf with dumb] she began the arduous task of teaching him herself. She refused to accept the fact that her son could not learn. She sang and talked to her son and tried to get him to associate sounds with meaning. She taught him to lip read and speak.[8] Her hard work paid off. John eventually graduated from college and had a successful career working as an illustrator for Disney Studios. Their story is a true testament to the limitless potential of a child. But it wasn't until 1942 that she created the John Tracy Clinic because she was contacted by several mothers desperate to help their deaf children and recognized her success with John.[9] Mrs. Tracy dedicated the rest of her life to helping children with hearing loss to learn. If Mrs.

---

8. John Tracey Clinic
9. Louise Treadwell Tracy Blessed Among Women Article by Suzanne Woods Fisher

Tracy had listened to the "experts" of her time, her son John would have remained in a truly silent world.

There is no direct statement on the District's part regarding Max's potential to learn, but I believe this theme underscored every decision. Descriptions of Max "progressing nicely" during his Sea Cliff School years were replaced with terms like "progressing slow and steady" and "some progression." It didn't take me long to figure out these phrases meant absolutely nothing. Teachers and administrators would recite these words at CSE meetings and Impartial Hearings like trained seals but they were just words used to market Max for whatever outcome the District wanted. I knew Max would progress if only the right way was found but I didn't feel the District shared my point of view. In future Impartial Hearings, every time I heard a teacher state Max was "progressing slowly" as a means for the District to avoid reading services they were telling me my son did not have the potential to learn. That this was all I could ever expect from him.

Max was effectively a clean slate at the age of nine, abandoned by his current school and entering the third grade in the fall at the School for Language and Communication Development (SLCD), the out of district placement with the dubious label of a non-reader with memory issues and a learning disability. The odds were not in his favor; Max was three years behind his peers, losing ground each day and no one seemed to be able to get this kid to read. I was incredibly fearful of Lindamood-Bell's ability to succeed where the District failed. Max would be placed in Lindamood-Bell's Seeing Stars Program the summer before he began SLCD. The Seeing Stars Program focuses on decoding, spelling and speech issues to counter effect weak phonemic awareness.[10] Phonemic awareness is the ability

---

10. www.lindamoodbell.com

to distinguish sounds (phonemes) in spoken language and how they relate to written language. Phonemic awareness is considered vital to the early stages of literacy.[11]

Their goal for Max utilizing this program for the eight weeks was a one year gain in reading in areas of sight word recognition and decoding. This point needs to be clarified because there are many components to reading: phonemic awareness, phonics, reading fluency, vocabulary development and comprehension. This program provides the building blocks to begin the process by helping children learn the very basics. It essentially gives them the foundation on which to build the more complicated aspects of reading.

I felt as though Lindamood-Bell was a last resort for Max. If this didn't work, we had no other options and this was a frightening reality. I had pushed for it, fought for it and if it didn't work there was no one else to blame. I would sit alone at night without the distractions of the day and worried if I was making the right decisions for Max. Sometimes, I would wake from a sound sleep and run to the bathroom sick to my stomach. My fear for Max was that if he didn't make any progress with Lindamood-Bell the District would pigeonhole him for the rest of his educational career.

Right before Max began his instruction at Lindamood-Bell I had another meeting with Carl Martin who walked me through the process and what Max would be doing on a day to day basis. He then introduced me to a young woman named Noreen and explained that she would be Max's coordinator. As coordinator she was responsible for overseeing Max's program and making adjustments to ensure Max was getting the most benefit out of the program.

---

11. www.wisegeek.com

Noreen was friendly and took the time to talk to me about the program and my concerns.

I couldn't wait for Max's first day at Lindamood-Bell but unfortunately I could not be there for him. He started on a Monday so Patrizia had the kids. I called Patrizia immediately after he was released from his session to find out how it went. I wanted details and specifics but all she has to say was, "He's okay and everything seemed to be fine." I would have to wait until tomorrow when I brought Max to Lindamood-Bell to get the answers I sought.

Tuesday couldn't come fast enough. I was on pins and needles waiting to hear what Noreen had to say. I am not sure what I was expecting after only two days in the program. When Noreen came out after her session with Max, I was slamming her with one question after another. "How is he doing?" "Is he getting anything?" "Is he learning?" "What's going on?" Noreen was very calm and responded to each one of my questions with great patience. She explained that Max had learned almost 50 sight words and understood the difference between consonants and vowels.

On the car ride home, Max was visibly excited and could not stop talking about all the things he had learned. He recited the vowels and told me they were different from the other letters. I was beside myself with joy as I listened and watched Max. The look of excitement on Max's face as he told me all about the letters and spelling words in the air sent chills though me. I told him how proud I was that he knew the letters and Max kept repeating "I know it, I know it" with the hugest smile on his face. The whole ride home I kept calling out words and he would spell them in the air. It was truly a joyful triumphant moment.

Thursday afternoon, Noreen invited me to stay and

watch the session; I eagerly accepted. I watched her work with Max as he was writing words in the air. Max was telling Noreen what letters make what sounds. Max was enjoying working with Noreen but more importantly, He was learning. By the end of the week Max knew the alphabet. Once again during the car ride home he happily displayed his new skills telling me about the letters and reciting the alphabet. This was the first time I ever saw Max excited about anything related to reading. All of my doubts about Lindamood-Bell's ability were squelched by the end of the first week.

By the end of second week, I cautiously attempted to get Max to read with me on the couch. I remember the look of sheer horror on Ryan's face as I offered up *The Gingerbread Man* to Max. Obviously recalling the tirades of the past, she was waiting for the drama to begin...much to our surprise Max happily joined me on the couch and we proceeded to take turns reading. I was ecstatic that Max was making major progress on the Seeing Stars Program but this only fueled my anger with the District. Max's success at Lindamood-Bell left no doubt in my mind that the District was negligent and had damaged my son.

The summer program was intensive, five days a week for four hours a day. Max made some major sacrifices that summer. He didn't get to visit his grandparents with his sister; he didn't get to go to summer camp. Max spent the majority of his summer working on reading. From the beginning it was obvious that this program clicked with Max. Week after week I watched him excel and it was thrilling for me to watch my son begin the process that would enable him to read. Entering Lindamood-Bell was a turning point for Max and it provided me with a tremendous sense of relief. The two year knot in my stomach had finally loosened. Halfway through the program Max exceeded Lindamood-Bell's expectations and he was nominated for "Student of The Year." I was shocked to learn he didn't win and couldn't imagine that another kid actually made more strides than Max but it didn't matter. All that mattered was that we found a way to teach Max. The best part of the whole experience was that Max understood his accomplishment. He was proud to be able to read and enjoyed learning at Lindamood-Bell.

By the end of his fourth week, I took Max to a Barnes & Noble to buy him some books to celebrate. After we worked our way to the children's section, I watched as he pulled *Green Eggs and Ham* off the shelf. We sat at a table and he began to read the first paragraph. When he was finished, I positioned myself to read the second paragraph keeping with our routine, but he stopped me and said, "No. I'll read." Max spent the next forty five minutes reading the entire book to me just to show me he could do it. The store clerk came by and was amazed. She said "You should be proud." I replied with eyes glazed over, "This is the first book he has ever read to me."

During the last week of the program Max needed to take another evaluation similar to the one he had taken at the beginning of the summer. This time he completed the entire four hour test. When I met with Noreen to discuss the results, she showed me that Max made progress in every area. She told me that when she informed Max that he completed the final portion, he looked at her exhausted and ran his fingers through his hair and asked her if he could tell her something. She replied, "Yes" and he proceeded to tell her, "My daddy is my best friend and all I want to do is make him happy."

On Max's last day at Lindamood-Bell he received a certificate of completion for the Seeing Stars Program and the

Dr. Seuss book, *Oh! The Places You'll Go*. As I got close to Max I could see he was visibly upset so I knelt down and asked, "Hey buddy, what's wrong?" Max looked at me with tears in his eyes and said, "I really like this place, they help me, everybody is nice to me; I want to come back." As I looked up at Noreen I saw she was turning to walk away. It was clear she was starting to cry so I let her go. I looked back at Max and told him, "Don't worry I will get you back here, I promise." Max smiled and gave me a hug.

I concluded two very important things from Max's experience at Lindamood-Bell:

- The right teaching approach will enable a child to learn.

- Children have endless potential.

> **Second Year at Sea Cliff School**
> **10 Month School Year**
>
> Carol Speranza, Reading Teacher, Wilson Reading Program
> One-on-one, 30 minutes, Five Days a Week
>
> Karen Demeo, Speech & Audiologist, 30 minutes, Five Days a Week
>
> | | |
> |---|---|
> | 10-month school year | Approximately 50 Sight Words and doesn't know the alphabet or sounds of the letters. |

Lindamood-Bell
Eight Weeks - Seeing Stars Program

Week One	60 sight words – 50 sight words are stabilized. Max knew single sounds of consonants. Two sound words (it, at, go) three sound words (zip, pat, lit).
Week Two	85 sight words – 75 sight words are stabilized. Vowel sounds are stabilized. Max knew the difference between vowels and consonants. Max was introduced to phonics readers.
Week Three	135 sight words – 125 sight words are stabilized. Max is decoding words with blends (plan, point, spoon).
Week Four	185 sight words – 175 sight words are stabilized. Five sound words (frost, plant). Max exceeds Lindamood-Bells goal.
Week Five	210 sight words – 200 sight words are stabilized. Max is reading 1st grade paragraphs. Introduction: multi-syllable concepts.
Week Six	235 sight words – 225 sight words are stabilized. Introduction: common affixes (ture, tion) re-enforcement: rapid decoding – independent decoding.
Week Seven	260 sight words – 250 sight words are stabilized. Two syllable decoding. Increase fluency 1st grade level.
Week Eight	275 sight words – 265 sight words are stabilized. Stabilize – syllables, affixes. Max takes a four hour test. Test results show improvement in all areas with some over a two-year gain.

Max's success at Lindmood-Bell confirmed my belief that he did not suffer from any issues that prevented him from learning. It would have been impossible for him to make the gains he achieved in such a short period of time. Although, Noreen and the staff at Lindamood-Bell were able to work wonders with Max, the reality was that eight weeks were not going to make up for two years of the District's failures. Lindamood-Bell gave Max the gift of decoding but he still had a long road ahead of him. I would spend the next three years fighting to get Lindamood-Bell on Max's IEP.

5
The Chairperson Rules

"Experts often have more data than judgment"
Colin Powell

I IMMEDIATELY SET UP A CSE MEETING in August to request that the one-on-one remedial reading services of Lindamood-Bell be placed on Max's IEP for his upcoming third grade school year. I had two major strikes against me. The District made it crystal clear it did not want to place an unapproved program on the IEP and IDEA does not direct school districts to state methodology on an IEP. A very simple definition of methodology is the way a teacher teaches. If Max's case proved anything to me, it was that methodology is vital to teaching children with disabilities, and I wasn't going to let the District or the law stop me.

Early on Max was evaluated as a student who would benefit from a multisensory approach to teaching reading. This is defined as an approach that uses all the learning pathways: seeing, hearing, feeling, and awareness of motion, brought together by the thinking brain.[12] The problem is there are many multisensory reading approaches: Wilson Reading Program, Orton-Gillingham, Recipe for Reading and Lindamood-Bell are examples. Wilson Reading Program[13] and Recipe for Reading[14] are based

---

12. www.ortonacademy.org
13. www.wilsonlanguage.com
14. www.eps.schoolspecialty.com

on the Orton-Gillingham approach which is a highly recognized scientifically based methodology that is utilized primarily for dyslexia. Lindamood-Bell is not based on Orton-Gillingham but it is also a scientifically based method.[15] Congress requires the child's IEP to include "a statement of special education, related services and supplementary aids and services, based on peer reviewed research …" (Section 1414(d)(1)(A))[16]. All of these programs technically qualify so as long as the District offered any multisensory approach it felt its job was complete but I held a different opinion. Max was a deaf child who relied heavily on vision to acquire information, additionally, he was classified as a "visual learner" as a result of the WISC4 (Wechsler Intelligence Scale for Children 4th edition) which was administered by the District. Lindamood-Bell unlike the other approaches is unique because it utilizes mental imagery as a means to learn making it a highly visual approach. Lindamood-Bell resonated with Max's needs and he did well on the program making it the appropriate method. Max was entering SLCD and his teachers were not trained in the Lindamood-Bell approach so he would be exposed to new approaches that may not work for him. This was unacceptable to me.

The CSE Meeting proved to be a battle of wills between the District and me. Carl Martin from Lindamood-Bell attended the meeting and spoke at length about Max's success on the program and what their programs could achieve if he continued. I showed them test results from Lindamood-Bell showing Max's jump in decoding. I highlighted all of Max's achievements; he knew the alphabet, the sounds of the letters and had mastered 265 sight words but the District would not be swayed. The District stated that they could not place Lindamood-Bell on the IEP because it was not an approved program. Tom Korb further added that the reading programs offered

---

15. www.lindamood-bell.com
16. www.wrightlaw.com

5: The Chairperson Rules

by SLCD supplied FAPE and that Max did not need to continue with any one-on-one remedial reading. So not only did the District shoot down my suggestion to use Lindamood-Bell, they made it clear that they wouldn't be utilizing any one-on-one reading services for Max, approved or not. I could not understand the District's resistance. I felt the District owed Max a chance to catch up. I couldn't believe that Tom Korb could sit across a table from me and speak these words. Once again, I was forced to sit for hours through a CSE meeting and listen to the District praise the programs SLCD offered (Recipe for Reading and Milestone for Reading) and the other services they were going to provide.

Scared out of my mind that I wouldn't find a way to educate Max; Lindamood-Bell was more than I had hoped. I wholeheartedly felt that Lindamood-Bell was the answer I was seeking. Now that I found the way through sheer luck, a bigger problem loomed over Max. It turns out that finding the way was only the beginning; it was getting the School District to agree on the way that would prove to be the biggest battle I would face. I am now a Special Education Administrator's worst nightmare, a parent whose child experienced success with an unapproved program outside of the District. I wasn't just going to sit by when I felt the District was jerking around with my son's future. Lindamood-Bell's approach afforded Max an opportunity to make up for two lost years. Max needed to continue with the remedial reading services in addition to his programs at SLCD. I would not compromise Max's education any longer.

The CSE process was not working for me. IDEA states that schools must invite parents to CSE meetings and that parental participation must be more than mere formality. As a parent I am legally allowed to represent Max's best interest and give input I feel is relevant to his education. Max's success on the Lindamood-Bell program was a telling outcome so I presented facts (test scores) combined with Mr. Martin's clarification of the program and why it worked, but it didn't matter. The District listened politely and then proceeded to do exactly as it pleased. Going forward, all CSE meetings would follow this format. I would show up, present facts and even have teachers and Max's speech therapist from SLCD speak to the benefit of Lindamood-Bell but the results were always the same. The District Chairperson had absolute veto power and would completely shut me down. I was essentially invited to a process in which I had no real say. It is an incredibly frustrating, heart wrenching experience to have no control over a situation that affects your child.

The District could make any argument it wanted for not putting Lindamood-Bell on the IEP and there wasn't anything I could do about it. Their decision to forgo a proven method for Max and utilize programs that may not work wasn't a gamble I was willing to take. At this point, I didn't give any credence to what the District thought. If I sat back and waited for these "educators" to educate my son he'd be thirty still learning his ABCs. After the CSE meeting ended, I quickly filed for my third Impartial Hearing.

During this time, I felt my last two encounters with the District were successful, getting the outside consultant on the IEP and getting the settlement agreement so I may have been over-confident going into this particular battle. It wasn't until my third Impartial Hearing began that I realized what actually happened and my confidence about my wins were shattered. In the end, I believe I was taken advantage of by the District.

5: The Chairperson Rules

The District admitted Sea Cliff School was not an appropriate placement, offered no immediate remedy and wanted Max to wait four months to find an appropriate placement. The District was in violation of IDEA. Keeping a child in an inappropriate placement while it figures things out is not providing FAPE. Did Mr. Korb scramble to protect himself and the budget by doing a little damage control offering a bogus settlement agreement? Yes, I made a mistake signing the settlement agreement when I should have pressed for more reading services but it doesn't negate that Mr. Korb knowingly made a deal where an eight year old deaf child would suffer and played on my fears as a father putting me in a damned if I do damned if I don't situation. And then to add insult to injury, the District offered less compensation under the guise of administrative costs for making them go through the expense of an Impartial Hearing. What about the cost to Max? I guess it didn't matter to them. The District basically killed two birds with one stone by saving money on services and placing a gag order on me, stunting my ability to represent my son at future Impartial Hearings.

The aftermath of signing the settlement agreement was catastrophic to my argument at the third Impartial Hearing. The settlement agreement covered the entire school year 2007/2008. It made it impossible to compare Max's success on the Lindamood-Bell program summer 2008 versus the prior school 2007/2008 when I wasn't allowed to bring up that timeframe. Every time, I mentioned those dates, Attorney Gibson kept accusing me of wanting to, "take another bite of the apple" because I was discussing things that had already been settled. And the Impartial Hearing Officer, Esta Mora agreed. How could I show Max needed the Lindamood-Bell program when I couldn't bring his most recent educational records into the hearing? The advocate philosophy of "get whatever you can get now and get more later" wasn't working for me.

I felt like I signed a deal with the devil and every time I tried to help my son, Attorney Gibson was throwing the settlement agreement in my face. I couldn't make a right move for Max. Nobody was playing fair! I couldn't believe these people were in the business of educating children. Their behavior reflected the kind of things I associated with slumlords, criminals, societal bottom feeders, people who basically use the law to defend their illegal behavior. Not educators! Their behavior didn't just baffle me, it disgusted me.

The Impartial Hearing dragged on for three months, October 2008 thru December 2008 and it wasn't looking good for Max. It was extremely hard for me to make my case without all the relevant information. It was infuriating.

To make matter worse, the testimony of his teachers at Sea Cliff did not help my case. Ms. Speranza testified that Max knew approximately 50 sight words at the end of his second grade year but when asked about Max's ability to read words on a second grade level after attending Lindamood-Bell she stated that he was not reading at a 2.8 grade level because he did not comprehend the material at this level. As far as decoding goes he was recognizing sight words and able to read books. Nobody claimed that he understood the material on a second grade level.[17] The significance of him decoding on a second grade level was diminished as a result.

Ms. Roberts' testimony was equally disappointing. At the end of the previous summer Max and I ran into

---

17. (Impartial Hearing Testimony, December 10,2008 page 503 lines 20-23)

5: The Chairperson Rules

Ms. Roberts when I had to drop off some paperwork at the school. She was in one of the classrooms and I offered to show her how much Max had improved in reading. She didn't have the book I requested so I told her to grab any book off the shelf. Max read a paragraph and she seemed absolutely amazed he was reading with no problems and following the words along with his fingers. She commented how nicely Max was coming along and that he knew the words. But during her testimony when I questioned her about our visit and Max's reading ability she stated that Max's reading was not consistent so it was hard to say if Lindamood-Bell helped at all. When I asked her if she saw a difference between how Max was reading after Lindamood-Bell compared to his reading during the previous school year, she stated, "I have to state that was not a consistent thing. There were days when he would read like that, and there were days that he couldn't. So I did see that reading at times in the classroom."

Fortunately, Ms. Bitner, Max's teacher at SLCD was very forthcoming in her testimony regarding her take on implementing IEPs. At the time of the hearing I didn't fully understand the impact of her testimony but it would turn out to be Max's saving grace.[18] I was simply too focused on Max's teachers from Sea Cliff that I failed to realize the significance. The testimonies of Carol Speranza and Ms. Roberts bewildered me and I couldn't figure out how to make an argument against them. The District seemed to have the perfect defense. The teachers had problems educating Max because he had a memory issue and they had a hard time determining his academic standing because he wasn't a consistent student.

The Impartial Hearing officer gave the District and me

---

18. (Impartial Hearing Testimony, October 28, 2008 pages 370 -373)

75

thirty days to file our closing briefs and said she would send the decision within two weeks. The closing brief is a written document stating a party's position on the matter and can include facts, allegations and case law. This was my first time writing a brief and I had no idea what I was doing. I just wrote from the heart, stated my case and hoped for the best. I sent my brief in as soon as possible even though I knew the District's attorney would use all the allotted days. I didn't receive the Impartial Hearing decision until February 7, 2009. I wasn't surprised when I read that the Impartial Hearing Officer decided in favor of the School District. The Hearing Officer along with the District cut my evidence down to nothing under the faux pretense of "rearguing FAPE." Max's entire second grade year where he made minimal progress versus the eight weeks at Lindamood-Bell were not spoken of during the Hearing. It was sheer negligence to me that the Impartial Hearing Officer could just ignore pertinent educational information about a student.

Now, I had to move quickly. This process was already taking too long. I had to file an appeal with the State Review Officer (SRO) costing Max more time. The State Review Officer is supposed to evaluate the decisions of the Impartial Hearing Officers, look at the evidence: testimony and other relevant documents that are part of the hearing and make a decision whether or not the Impartial Hearing decision will stand. I had thirty five days to file and the District had fourteen days to respond. The SRO had thirty days to make a decision once all the evidence was received.

This battle started in August, the Impartial Hearing dragged on until December and now I had to wait for the SRO decision. A whole school year was going by and Max's education was suffering. I had no faith in the system at all. I believed I was dealing with a bunch of spin doctors

5: The Chairperson Rules

from the District saying anything and everything but the truth and an Impartial Hearing Officer that in my opinion was District oriented. I was not sure what course of action I would take if the SRO also decided with the District. Federal Court or just admit defeat? Both options were not good. I couldn't relax until I had the SRO decision.

The letter from the SRO finally arrived one evening, late April 2009. I was out on a date with a girl I was seeing, JoAnn. I had explained to her a little about what was going on with Max but she had no real understanding of what was really involved. I figured if the relationship lasted there would be enough time to get into the details. I checked the mail religiously each day looking for the letter and tonight was no different. Reaching into the mailbox, I pulled out a handful of mail. JoAnn was waiting to get into my apartment and was probably wondering why I was sorting the mail outside in the dark on a bitter cold night when I suddenly found the letter I sought. The SRO decision was in my hands and nothing else mattered. I ran up the stairs leaving JoAnn in the driveway. I ran into the living room and turned on the lights to read it. JoAnn followed behind, asking what happened, sensing my urgency. I shook her off, and kept reading until I found the decision. "The Appeal is sustained…" the SRO went on to say "It is ordered…" and "It is further ordered…" and so on… all I saw was… Max won!

It wasn't until later on that JoAnn got a full understanding of what was happening and why I was fighting with the District. It wouldn't take long for her to become fully engrossed in what was happening; reading special education law and trying to make sense of the system. She would quickly become as frustrated as I was trying to understand why the District made the choices it did in regards to Max. She would help me with all future dealings with the District.

Although, the State Review Officer (SRO) decided that the District was providing Max an appropriate education with the IEP offered, Ms. Bitner's testimony proved fatal. Ms. Bitner testified she did not read the IEP and this was a major procedural error the SRO could not ignore. The SRO overturned the Hearing Officer's decision and instructed that another CSE meeting was to take place and all parties should decide together on a reading program which would be implemented no later than thirty days after the date of the decision, April 22, 2009.

Before the CSE meeting, Patrizia had suggested we tape it, something we hadn't done in the past. She wrote a letter to SLCD requesting that they tape the meeting on our behalf and the school agreed. The CSE meeting was extremely tense and I think everyone in the room was on edge. Mr. Korb was chairing the meeting and by now I sensed I was not one of his favorite parents. But it gave me great satisfaction to sit across from him knowing he had to give me exactly what he didn't want, one-on-one reading services. When I asked if they had a reading service to offer Max, his answer was a simple, "No. We are trying to figure it out." And then he stated oddly, "This is not what this meeting is for." I was mystified since this was the sole purpose of the meeting as directed by the SRO decision. I pressed forward and suggested utilizing Lindamood-Bell but he refused. When I pushed for a reason, he stated, "Because I don't have to!" I honestly don't think Mr. Korb remembered the session was being taped. I believe this fight had become personal for him and he let his guard down. The tension in the room escalated and nobody was speaking. Needless to say, nothing was accomplished and nobody walked away happy.

5: The Chairperson Rules

A day or so later, I got a call from Mr. Korb whose solution was reading services provided by Ms. Speranza using the Wilson Reading Program. I couldn't believe he would suggest Ms. Speranza. Why would I agree to expose Max to a situation that didn't work in the past? Additionally, the Wilson Program was not an appropriate approach for Max who needed help with comprehension not decoding. The Wilson Reading Program was going to be the issue. The District had plenty of teachers who could provide the reading services so I had to move fast on discrediting Wilson as an appropriate program.

I called Wilson and spoke with a representative, Mark Foran who agreed that it was not an appropriate program for Max. I wrote a letter to Tom Korb explaining my discussion with the Wilson representative. I also had an unlikely ally on my side. Ronnie Glass, the Speech and Audiologist from SLCD who agreed that Lindamood-Bell was the approach that worked with Max. She was extremely helpful in researching the differences in Wilson Reading Programs vs. Lindamood-Bell and wrote a page long letter detailing why she felt Lindamood-Bell was the right method with research attached. I sent both letters to Mr. Korb who still would not agree to use Lindamood-Bell.

The school year had come and gone without the reading services. On May 22, 2009, I filed for my fourth Impartial Hearing for the school year, 2009/2010 to request that Lindamood-Bell be placed on Max's IEP for his fourth grade year. My attitude at this point was if the District didn't want to spend federal funds on special education services for my son then I felt compelled to make them spend money on attorney fees. I also followed up with a complaint against Mr. Korb to the New

York State Education Department for not conducting a CSE in a fair matter as described by state and federal regulations and for not complying with a SRO order in a timely fashion. The SRO decision was dated April 22, 2009, it was now June and Max was still not receiving reading services. The District exceeded the thirty days.

Somewhere in the interim of my putting in the State Complaint, the District finally agreed to use Lindamood-Bell in compliance with the SRO order to provide reading services. I am not sure why the sudden about face on the District's part but I was relieved Max would attending Lindamood-Bell for summer reading services. Even more of a shock was that the District agreed to settle my fourth Impartial Hearing complaint before the hearing even started. Although, I cannot discuss the details, I felt it was a momentous victory for Max.

A short time later I got a call from Mr. Korb at home asking me to pull the State Complaint against the District. Was this a coincidence? I don't know but the timing was perfect. I told him, "No, I won't pull the complaint." and he proceeded to threaten me, "Wait until the next time you want something." My complaint with the state was sustained! The District was found in violation of NYCRR 200.4(f) - IEP regulations require that the concerns of the parent for enhancing the education of a child be discussed.

Why didn't I pull the complaint? I felt bullied by the District and Mr. Korb. His refusal to allow me to speak at a CSE meeting and his disregard for a SRO decision delayed my son's education. I didn't like Mr. Korb and felt his bullying needed to stop.

6
"Because I Don't Have To!"

"No man is above the law and no man is below it: nor do we ask any man's permission when we ask him to obey it."
Theodore Roosevelt

TOM KORB'S STATEMENT, "Because I don't have to" captured perfectly the overall attitude I came to associate with the Special Education industry which is that I had no business getting involved with my son's education. When I expressed concern that a consultant was needed during Max's first year in District I was told it wasn't necessary and was forced to file paperwork for an Impartial Hearing. When I expressed concern that Max wasn't making any gains early on his second grade year, his teachers assured me everything was fine. Max's second grade report card in the areas of reading, comprehension and writing were a static ranking of 1 (*Area of Concern*) the entire year but the District provided no alternative intervention. By May of his second grade year, the District wanted Max in an out of district placement and claimed they only realized there was a problem in the late winter/early spring and forced me to file for an Impartial Hearing for reading services. When I requested one-on-one reading services be continued, the District informed me that the services provided by SLCD was enough to supply FAPE. Ultimately, Max's SLCD teacher, Ms. Bitner admitted she didn't read the IEP denying Max FAPE. The SRO directed the District to work with me and decide on a reading service. I suggested a reading service and Mr. Korb flat out refused it. I had the overwhelming sense something more was at play. Were egos getting in the way of my son's education?

Reviewing the transcript to my third Impartial Hearing, the Officer, Esta Mora repeatedly questioned Ms. Bitner when she admitted that she didn't read the IEP. The Hearing Officer pointedly asked her, "Do you feel that you can deliver appropriate services without having reviewed his file?"[19]

Ms. Bitner answered, "I know what basically a third grade child in special ed. has to be taught. I feel that if I had to – I know basically what most IEP goals have been, after being a teacher for so many years."[20]

Ms. Bitner explained for a page and half in documented testimony how she didn't utilize the IEPs until grades were due on November 14th. She goes on further to explain that she's been teaching for years and has a good understanding of what the children need. (Note to Parents whose children attended SLCD school year 2008/2009 and were in Ms. Bitner's class – she testified she didn't utilize the IEPs until grades were due in November).[21] The Impartial Hearing Officer who is supposed to know and understand Special Education Law decided in favor of the School District. The Impartial Hearing Officer stated in her decision:

---

19. Impartial Hearing Testimony, October 28, 2008 page 370 lines 4-6
20. Impartial Hearing Testimony, October 28, 2009 page 370 lines 7-12
21 Impartial Hearing Testimony, October 28, 2008 pages 369-373

"A review of the hearing record establishes that the student is receiving FAPE. There is nothing in the record to indicate that there were procedural inadequacies which (a) impeded the student's right to FAPE, (c) caused a deprivation of educational benefit."

The IEP is a legally binding contract stating the education plan for an individual student. Did this teacher understand what the law required? How could a special education teacher think it was okay not to read the IEP? How can a teacher implement an IEP without reading it? And why would an Impartial Hearing Officer find this acceptable? Where opinions and preferences more important than the law? Where teachers and administrators able to be subjective on their own knowledge, abilities and methods and not take it personally when a parent says what they're doing isn't working? I wasn't out to insult the District or Max's teachers but it was obvious to me Max wasn't making gains for two years and the District wouldn't even discuss the possibility of seeking other avenues.

This Impartial Hearing Officer's decision shook my faith in the system even further. If I couldn't depend on the Impartial Hearing Officers to protect Max on definitive issues how could I expect them to evaluate ambiguous issues fairly? I also wasn't comfortable with Max attending SLCD any longer. I was spending a great deal of time and energy fighting for services and the correct goals to be placed on IEPs so for a teacher not to read it for two months was a disappointing discovery I had to think about. It made me question all special education teachers that came into contact with Max. Was Ms. Bitner's testimony, an unfortunate slip up for the District, really just an acceptable norm?

To make matters worse, I felt like I was the one looked

upon as unreasonable by people within the Special Education Industry. I was the loving parent who was being irrational about my son's education and potential while the professionals in the industry were viewed as rational, realistic and more informed. The "loving parent" a bias that exists within the Special Education Industry impart due to the U. S. Court of Appeals for the Second Circuit decision in a New York tuition reimbursement case, *Walczak v. Florida Union Free School District*. The Court found that the program proposed by the public school provided B. W. (the child) with a free appropriate education because schools do not have to provide the "best" education that loving parents want for their child, only what is appropriate. I felt like I had erroneously earned the stigma of "loving parent" and nobody wanted to look past it to what was really going on with Max's education. If I was guilty of being a "loving parent" what where the administrators, teachers, and Impartial Hearing Officers guilty of?

Yes, I love Max, but school personnel certainly have their own agendas which could possibly effect their decisions. Parents are attending CSE meetings and questioning school personnel on their abilities and methods which cannot be easy for anyone to hear; now add a budget on top of this and the combination could prove toxic for special education children. Even if a teacher does recognize that what they are doing may not be working for a particular child it is not a guarantee they will speak up on behalf of this child. And I do believe that most teachers want to help these children, but I don't think they will jeopardize their livelihood to do it. These are tough hurdles for parents to overcome.

District personnel have very precious things on the line:

- BUDGET

- JOB SECURITY

- TENURE

- WORK ENVIRONMENT

I do feel that a lot of teachers are intimated and are forced to make less than honest assessments of the services and goals. So parents are up against school administrators, teachers, school psychologists and specialists (i.e. speech pathologists, teachers of the deaf) holding master's degrees and doctorates who may not have a child's best interest at heart. No wonder so many parents don't bother fighting. School personnel throw out a few legal catch phrases and viola … **FAPE**!

"Progressing slowly"

"Reasonability calculated"

"Progressing to his/her potential"

My theory that school personnel were just saying whatever they needed to say to avoid giving Max the reading services was reinforced by the inconsistencies I noted when reading through several Impartial Hearings. Below are a few examples of these inconsistencies:

Impartial Hearing – June 26, 2008

Prior to this Impartial Hearing, Mr. Korb told me that Lindamood-Bell cannot be place on the IEP because it was not an approved program by New York State.

James Monk, Impartial Hearing Officer, stated "An unapproved program can be taken into consideration but only for very specific reasons." (Despite Mr. Monk's addressing this fallacy of non approved programs Mr. Korb still uses this excuse as part of his reasoning to deny Max the reading services). An unapproved program can be placed on an IEP as part of "related services" and is independent of special education. Related services enhance the benefit of special education and are not required to be implemented by certified special education teachers. And it has been done in other New York State school districts i.e. Roslyn School District. Please review NYS SRO Decision #02-025 where a Roslyn School District CSE meeting convened and place two periods a week of Lindamood-Bell Processing Center on the child's IEP. It appears that New York School Districts can place an unapproved program on a child's IEP if the District chooses to do it.

Impartial Hearing, October 2008 thru December 2008

Mr. Korb attempted to show the Impartial Hearing Officer, Esta Mora how accommodating the District is trying to be with a service but ends up contradicting himself. Mr. Korb explained that the District is allowing Max to be given speech therapy by Ronnie Glass who he mistakenly thinks is an unapproved provider. He stated, "That person was not contracted by the… <u>was not an approved provider.</u> But we immediately upon his request made .. very quickly, made whatever arrangements we needed to make in order to honor the parent's request."

And then later in his testimony regarding Lindamood-Bell, he states, "We do not put a non–state approved program on IEPs because they are not approved by New York State."

The District can use a non approved Speech Therapist but not a non-state approved reading program.

Mr. Korb also stated, "Methods are determined by classroom teachers."

Recipe for Reading, a program SLCD was utilizing to teach reading to Max was described by a SLCD Teacher as a multisensory reading program based on the Orton-Gillingham approach.

Impartial Hearing, July 2010

Marcy Laredo stated, "I cannot put a non-approved reading program on the IEP."

Marcy Laredo stated that a committee decides the teaching methodology contradicting Mr. Korb's statement from Impartial Hearing, 2008.

Attorney Gibson states that it hadn't been established that Orton-Gillingham was part of Recipe for Reading. It was established during the last Impartial Hearing and a major argument the District used to claim they were supplying FAPE.

I find this behavior deviant and I don't feel it is the norm for how educators should behave. A true educator would align themselves with the child and there is simply no evidence of this in my dealings with the North Shore School District. A true educator can stand back and state "What I am doing isn't working; I need help to educate this child." A true educator is curious about new methods and is willing to learn and adapt these methods. Institutions of learning should foster teacher learning and should never instill a closed door policy. The whole point of IDEA is to provide children with an IEP that is specifically designed to meet the unique needs of a child. An IEP cannot possibly meet the unique needs of a child under this inclusive philosophy school districts have adopted.

Teachers who go into CSE Meetings and Impartial Hearings and claim that an IEP is supplying FAPE when they know it isn't are committing perjury. School Administrators who put a budget before FAPE are breaking the law. If school administrators and teachers can run amuck saying and doing anything to support an agenda and the majority of "judges" are either willfully or ignorantly blinded by these presumptions of expertise and impartiality, then a child is basically screwed! Are they aware of the inconsistencies and just don't care because they get away with it? And why don't they care? Maybe, because it's easy not to care, get complacent or rationalize away this bad behavior due to a lack of accountability. Even when a Director of Special Education or a teacher or an Impartial Hearing Officer are found in violation of IDEA's procedural laws what remedy is taken to make sure that next time they do their job in accordance with the law? Maybe personnel in the field of Special Education would adhere to the law if they were held accountable in a meaningful way through disciplinary actions. Monetary fines with repeated offenses resulting in suspension and loss of wages. This would be a start.

North Shore School District and SLCD have repeatedly demonstrated that this combination is toxic to a child's academic success.

Max First Grade/Second Grade at Sea Cliff School

- Sea Cliff teachers, Beth LaWatsch, Lorraine Bedome and Carol Speranza could not teach Max the alphabet.

- Karen DeMeo, Speech Pathologist, could not get Max to understand the sounds of the letters.

- Sea Cliff School would not let Mill Neck Teacher, Ms. Dawson, transition Max into District and eventually banned her from the premises.

- Sea Cliff School never took any responsibility for Max's first two years in District making me fight for reading services.

Max's Third Grade Year at SLCD and My Third Impartial Hearing

- Tom Korb, Director of Special Education and Ms. Speranza visited Lindamood-Bell to review the program per my request it be placed on Max's 2008/2009 IEP. I learned during the Impartial Hearing that they both left after fifteen minutes. Both testified that 15 minutes was enough to understand how the program works and whether it was appropriate for the IEP.

- During the Impartial Hearing, Ms. Speranza was brought in as an expert witness for the District commenting on Lindamood-Bell test results despite the fact she has no training in the Lindamood-Bell programs.

Max's Fourth Grade Year at SLCD and My Sixth Impartial Hearing

- ◆ SLCD's "closed door policy" would not meet personnel from Lindamood-Bell face-to-face despite the fact that Lindamood-Bell made up a major component of Max's education.

- ◆ It is rumored that SLCD has an unwritten policy not to recommend outside services. Ronnie Glass testified that she has never seen the paperwork for this purpose used. She has only seen it in the orientation packet for parents.

- ◆ Max's SLCD teachers do not have reading certificates and received no formal training in the reading programs they were utilizing. Their claims that they were trained in reading programs are therefore questionable.

7
Teacher Training Is Fundamental

"You don't have to think too hard when you talk to teachers."
Jerome David Salinger (1919-2010)

MAX'S FIRST YEAR AT **SLCD** (third grade) without the Lindamood-Bell Services was another lost year. He seemed to plateau, making minimal gains in reading. During Max's fourth grade year he attended SLCD and Lindamood-Bell for one-on-one reading services three times a week for two hours a day. Lindamood-Bell reintroduced Max to the Seeing Stars Program and was able to provide a more in-depth instruction of the program. As Max progressed on the Seeing Stars program, Lindamood-Bell transitioned him to their Visualization and Verbalization for Language Comprehension and Thinking program. This program focuses on comprehension and critical thinking by stimulating concept imagery.[22] Although, Max was not able to complete this program because his hours ran out he made strides in all areas of reading: decoding, spelling, phonics and comprehension. But, Max was still not close to grade level in the area of comprehension which was at a dismal 2.5

---

22. www.lindamoodbell.com

grade level. He still needed a great deal of help with reading fluency and comprehension.

All the research I came across regarding literacy and children with disabilities indicated that placing them appropriately from the beginning was absolutely critical. The District's refusal to move Max into an appropriate placement or seek any type of intervention as soon as he wasn't making progress at Sea Cliff School damaged Max in ways I didn't want to imagine. I believe the District denied my son an appropriate placement. I believe the District knows how their lack of action affected the evolution of Max's education up and until present day. I believe the District refuses what he needs even though it was a direct result of their negligence and used and still uses unethical measures to avoid placing Lindamood-Bell services on the IEP. I believe all these things about the District but I still have to go through with the artifice of CSE meetings. When I entered the conference room to discuss Max's fifth grade IEP to request Lindamood-Bell, I knew I was going to have to file for an Impartial Hearing. A technique I mastered very early on was to have the paper semi filled out for the next step to hasten the process. I would print out and prepare paperwork in advance so I was ready to serve the school for an Impartial Hearing or file an appeal within 24 hours. It was the only recourse I had to speed up a process that was chipping away at Max's education.

Tom Korb was not present at the CSE meeting. The District sent Marcy Laredo, the Assistant Director of Special Education in Mr. Korb's place as the chairperson and she brought with her the following District personnel: Eric Fazioli, Assistant Director of Special Education, Megan Lang, Teacher of the Deaf, Mr. McKee, North Shore School Psychologist, Ms. Schielfman, regular class room teacher and a parent member. The parent member is a person who has experience attending CSE meetings due to their own child receiving special education services or at some point in the past received them. Their role is essentially to help walk the parents through the CSE process. Parents can decline a parent member's attendance simply by writing a request to their School District. I didn't need help with the process so the parent members at previous CSE meetings were usually silent attendees. I had never had a problem so I didn't oppose the District bringing the parent member to this meeting.

SLCD personnel included Ronnie Glass, Speech and Audiologist, Dana Matinale, Special Education Teacher, Ms. Lee, SLCD Psychologist. Patrizia and I both attended. Initially, I didn't understand why Ms. Laredo would bring along Mr. Fazioli or Mr. McKee since the roles were redundant. SLCD had brought a psychologist and why would Ms. Laredo need another Assistant Director to attend the meeting? Then I got my answer. Ms. Laredo instituted "polling" as a means to decide services. She claimed she wanted to get a consensus and asked everybody whether they agreed or disagree with services and counted the votes. People in the room were voting even though they had no contact with Max including the parent member. All the services provided in-house by SLCD received a resounding "yes" from District personnel (including the parent member) and all their votes for Lindamood-Bell service received a foreseeable "no." Patrizia and I naturally voted "yes" for Lindamood-Bell and his teachers from SLCD also supported the services. Ronnie Glass, Ms. Matinale and Ms. Lee all voted yes to the services continuing. Everyone involved with Max on a day-to-day basis in a teaching capacity voted for Lindamood-Bell and all personnel from the District who didn't have daily contact with Max voted "no." I wasn't happy.

To aggravate the situation, the parent member not

only voted against the services but she was argumentative when I questioned her taking part in the voting. She defended her actions and stated that she didn't know if she was right or wrong but she didn't think the services should continue. What kind of reasoning was this to vote against services for a disabled child? Then she told me I should, "see how he does without the services." Max's third grade year was a perfect example of how he did without the services so I was well aware of how he did without them. My son's education was not an experiment. Every opportunity this District had to prove to me they could educate Max on their own they failed. This parent member was not qualified to vote on services.

I was completely blindsided by the polling method and thought it was a new low for the District. I understood the District didn't want to put Lindamood-Bell on the IEP but this particular method of refusal was so unseemly. If I knew services were going to be decided by such a haphazard method I would have brought additional people with me as well."[23] It is not appropriate to make IEP decisions based upon a majority vote (34 CFR 300). When I expressed my distaste for the polling method and the unfairness of this whole meeting Ms. Laredo replied, "Well, it's in my right and this is the way I choose to do it."[24] I was promptly informed by one of her District allies, Mr. Fazioli that I could seek an Impartial Hearing. This was this particular District's solution to any conflict, no compromise, just deny the service by any means necessary and head straight to an Impartial Hearing. How can a parent compete with a District who refuses a service even when three teachers recommend it? Did the District (who can meet with teachers beforehand) know this was going to be a problem going into this meeting and stacked the vote?

---

23. CSE Meeting Tape
24. CSE Meeting Tape

The District had a history of not supplying FAPE in regards to Max's education and getting caught. I could only hope personnel would continue to trip up as I pressed on with my sixth Impartial Hearing. Even though I knew it would escalate to another hearing I couldn't help but be upset as I went home defeated. JoAnn and I grew closer over the months and she became my constant sounding board, listening and advising me on all issues with the District including this new development. As I prepared for this Impartial Hearing, she was by my side offering to help in any way she could. JoAnn and I put together the questions that I would ask each witness and reviewed what the witnesses should say to each question. JoAnn found case laws to support our position. Every day I would get e-mails from JoAnn with documents that supported our reasoning for Lindamood-Bell.

The following were my arguments during the Impartial Hearing and testimony gathered as a result of the hearing I felt supported my case:

Reading 20 U.S.C 1414 (d) (3) (A)(1) The IEP is the core of the statute and should be developed with both the strengths of the child in mind and concerns for parents enhancing the education of their child. Max's strength as a visual learner was not considered by the IEP team and they did not address a visualization approach parents believed had and will continue to tap into his strength as a visual learner enhancing his education. During the Impartial Hearing, Dr. Perez, a psychologist from the District confirmed that as a result of the WISC4 (administered by the District) that on his perceptual reasoning score; Max Gibson is more of a "visual learner."[25] Mr. Martin from LindaMood-Bell also testified that Max is a visual learner and this is how he learns best.[26] Ronnie Glass stated that reading is consid-

---

25. Impartial Hearing July 15, 2010 page 140 lines 15-19
26. Impartial Hearing July 20, 2010 page 445 lines 5-6

7: Teacher Training Is Fundamental

ered an auditory skill which makes it especially difficult for a deaf child like Max to master given that most reading programs are auditory.[27] Ronnie Glass described Max's progress his third grade year (with SLCD only) in the areas of reading as "minimal progress" while the following year with Lindamood-Bell she stated Max made, "more progress than he had the previous year in the area of reading and the area of comprehension."[28] Then Ms. Glass spoke to LindaMood-Bell's program Visualizing and Verbalization which uses mental imagery, as a well known approach in speech and language and it was the right kind of therapy to use a visualizing and verbalizing approach especially for a child who is hearing impaired and is very visual. She also stated that SLCD could not provide the same type of program. She went on to say, "He is doing well. He is improving with it." "To stop it at this point, not quite at grade level, I think is like cutting him off before he is finished."[29]

The District committed a procedural violation during the CSE meeting by refusing to consider Lindamood-Bell as a workable methodology. In Zachary Deal vs. Hamilton County Dept. of Educ.(2004), it was determined that the school district committed a procedural violation by refusing to consider Lovaas style ABA as workable methodology for the child's IEP. Please note that at the time of this decision "ABA" was not a state approved program, but is now a widely acceptable method for teaching autistic children. The parents of this child learned the program of "ABA" and taught this child at home. The parents were not certified special education teachers but judgment ruled they should be compensated for hours utilizing "ABA" program from their home until at least one expert in and advocate for Lovaas style

---

27. Impartial Hearing July 15, 2010 P 338
28. Impartial Hearing July 20120 page 332 lines 2-10
29. Impartial Hearing July 20, 2010 page332 lines 11-24/333 lines 2, 3, 7,8-11). (IHCT July 15, 2010 page 333 Ls 3, 4, 5)

7: Teacher Training Is Fundamental

ABA has developed an IEP for the child, Zachary that included at least 30 hours per week of Lovaas style ABA. A private placement is proper under IDEA if the education provided in the private placement is reasonably calculated to enable the child to receive an educational benefit. Knable, 238 F.3d at 770 (citing Florence County, 510) U.S. at 11).[30]

My reasoning was that due to the District's repeated statements that Lindamood-Bell could not be placed on the IEP because it was not a state approved school. How could the District give Lindamood-Bell any real consideration if this was the District's mindset? Tom Korb and Marcey Laredo both stated this about Lindamood-Bell in the past. During the CSE meeting when Marcy Laredo "polled" services for Lindamood-Bell it was not a genuine effort. Ms. Laredo's decision regarding Lindamood-Bell was predetermined and my proof was when she stated later at the Impartial Hearing that Lindamood-Bell couldn't be placed on the IEP because it was not a state approved school. If she couldn't place the services on the IEP then why poll the services in the first place?

Further evidence was when Ronnie Glass testified that during the deposition with the District with herself and Ms. Matinale present, Marcey Laredo referred to Lindamood-Bell as a "commercial program" and went on further to explain that the school district had concerns about the length of time Max would be attending Lindamood-Bell as "forever" and "there would never be an endpoint."[31] These remarks by Ms. Laredo affirmed my belief that the District did not care about the damage caused to my son. I found her remarks to be cruel but helpful for my case. If this was how Ms. Laredo felt

---

30. www.wrightlaw.com
31. Imparting Hearing July 15, 2010 P339 L22 and P344 Lines 2, 5 and 8).

about Max and Lindamood-Bell was she really giving my concerns for Max's education any real consideration at the CSE meeting?

There were also other things that came to light during the Impartial Hearing that solidified my belief that the District did not provide FAPE beyond my quest for Lindamood-Bell's Visualizing and Verbalizing program.

Through Ms. Matinale's testimony, I learned that Max aged out of the Recipe for Reading Program and was switched to the Wilson Reading Program. I couldn't believe that SLCD would not only switch him to a different program without consulting his parents but would use a program their own personnel, Ronnie Glass described as "counterproductive." I felt this particular decision on SLCD's part was damaging to the District's argument that FAPE was supplied. I still had the letter from Ronnie Glass which stated that Wilson's Reading Program was not appropriate for Max because it focused more on decoding and Max needed help in comprehension. As additional evidence, I also had an evaluation from the Beth Israel Medical Center and Children's Hearing Institute, the place where Max gets his cochlear implant tested and remapped. The Institute has pioneered research, education, and therapeutic efforts to improve the lives of deaf children for over two and half decades.[32] Their evaluation of Max recommended the programs Lindamood-Bell or Recipe for Reading for reading enhancement. The District and SLCD both had copies of this evaluation as part of Max's educational records. When Max aged out of the Recipe for Reading program, SLCD reading teachers should have used the other recommended reading program, Lindamood-Bell instead of utilizing Wilson. I could not understand how this

---

32. www.childrenshearingorg.org

happened. Were SLCD personnel not communicating with each other or were SLCD teachers aware of Ronnie Glass' letter and this evaluation and simply chose to ignore both because they had no other in-house reading program to offer?

I asked Max's reading teachers, Ms. Danielson and Ms. Bambara technical questions about the reading programs they were using as a means to prove that Lindamood-Bell was the right method but the answers each provided suggested that Max may not have received FAPE as a direct result of their teaching skills. When President Bush amended IDEA 2004, he reasoned it was "to ensure that students with disabilities will have special education teachers with the skills and training to teach special education and their subject area," ID. *At S44.*, an IEP must be properly implemented (8 NYCRR 200.4 (e) (7); Application of a Child with a Disability, Appeal No. 08-087). In describing permissible uses of federal funds, IDEA 2004 includes "providing professional development to special and regular education teachers who teach children with disabilities based on scientifically based research to improve educational instruction." (Section 1411(e)(2)(C)(xi)).

IDEA requires that teachers have an understanding of the disability of the children in their charge and how it affects their ability to learn. This makes sense given that a special education teacher would be involved in designing/implementing an education plan around a child's particular disability which is the whole point of the IEP.

Although, Congress recognizes that teachers who teach special education need to be trained in scientifically based research methods and allow funds to be utilized for this purpose it is up to each state to decide how teachers are trained. New York State does not set any guidelines for special education teachers to be trained in these scientifically based research methods. Orton-Gillingham, Wilson Reading Program and Lindamood-Bell all offer classes and set requirements each believe are important before a teacher can implement their programs where children can receive an educational benefit. I wasn't sure how Special Education Teachers in New York could implement these programs in accordance with each child's IEP without any formal training.

Ms. Danielson was responsible for implementing the Wilson Reading Program and Recipe for Reading Program. Ms. Danielson, two years out of school at the time of this hearing, stated she only received one day training in the Wilson Reading Program at SLCD. She didn't know if the Orton-Gillingham method was associated with the reading programs she utilized (*Exhibit A*). I couldn't understand how she could implement the IEP correctly if she didn't know these basic truths about the programs. How could SLCD expect a novice teacher to teach a child with a low incident disability on one day of training? **Certainly, one needs a greater understanding of these programs to teach a room of disabled children than could be gleaned from one lousy day of training.**

Ms. Bambara's testimony was equally disturbing. When I asked her if she was certified in any reading programs she appeared confused and said, "I don't know what certified means." The special education teacher entrusted with teaching a deaf child reading comprehension doesn't know what certified means when asked if she is certified in any reading programs. To add insult to injury when I asked her how deaf children and hard of hearing children process information differently from hearing children she answered, "I think they would need repetition" (*Exhibit B*). I wondered what President Bush would think of Ms. Bambara's answers and if he would think she was "highly qualified" to teach disabled children. A deaf child is going to need repetition?

Deaf children rely primarily on vision to process information. They are visual learners by the very nature of their disability. Deaf children cannot experience "incidental learning" which makes up for 90% of the learning that normal hearing individuals experience. Incidental learning is the ability to constantly pick up information from your environment. Background conversations, the news on TV or a teacher addressing another child's questions in a classroom are all things Max cannot experience. He needs to be taught directly what other hearing children learn naturally.[33] Deaf children process information literally so they do not understand idiomatic expressions such a "don't cry over spilt milk." Deaf children have trouble with double negatives, multiple word meanings, etc.[34] I felt a Special Education Teacher responsible for teaching reading to a deaf child should have been able to speak intelligently regarding this subject matter. How Max acquires and processes information is vital to teaching him. Quite frankly, I thought Ms. Bambara's answer trivialized my son's disability as though mere repetition was going to aid my son in acquiring a complex skill such as reading. In addition to my initial arguments I now included teacher competency as part of my closing brief to the Impartial Hearing Officer.

---

33. Mainstreaming the Student Who is Deaf or Hard of Hearing, Melanie Doyle and Linda Dye 2002
34. Deaf Learners and Successful Cognitive Achievement, David S. Martin PH.D.

7: Teacher Training Is Fundamental

Exhibit A – Ms. Danielson Testimony

One-Day Training - Impartial Hearing Date: July 15, 2010

FACT: Wilson Reading Program and Recipe for Reading are based on the Orton-Gillingham principles of teaching reading.

Direct , Questions from the District's Attorney Gibson to Ms. Danielson

Question: Did you receive any Wilson Training?
Answer: Yes.
Question: How much training did you get?
Answer: I received it at SLCD. It was one-day training.

Cross, My Questions to Ms. Danielson.

Question: Do you know the Orton-Gillingham methodology?
Answer: Yes.
Question: Do you know what it was originally specifically designed for, what disability?
Answer: Deaf? No?
Question: Is Orton-Gillingham within Recipe for Reading as far as you know?
Answer: I don't know.
Question: Some programs use underlying methodologies, such as Orton-Gillingham…
Attorney Gibson: Objection.
Question: I want to know if Ms. Danielson knows if Orton-Gillingham is used within – that methodology is used with those reading programs?
Attorney Gibson: Objection.
Hearing Officer: I will let her answer.
Answer: I don't know.

Exhibit B – Ms. Bambara's Testimony

> **"I Don't Know What Certified Means" Impartial Hearing Date: July 15, 2010**
>
> Ms. Bambara is responsible for implementing the Milestones for Reading Program.
>
> <u>Cross: My Questions to Ms. Bambara</u>
>
> **Question**: Are you certified in any specific reading program?
> **Answer**: I'm not sure. I don't know.
> **Question**: You don't know if you are certified or not?
> **Answer**: I don't know what certified means. We did get training in Recipe for Reading in SLCD, and I did get some training in Wilson. I don't know if I have a certificate. I haven't seen it so I'm not going to say yes.
> **Question**: You know Recipe for Reading?
> **Answer**: I have taught it.
> **Question**: Are there underlying methodologies that are in Recipe for Reading?
> **Answer**: I'm not sure. I don't know what they are.
> **Question**: Do you understand the difference between how a deaf and hard of hearing child process information compared to a regular child?
> **Answer**: Yes.
> **Question**: How?
> **Answer**: Wait, say it again. Can you repeat the question?
> **Question**: Sure. Do you understand the difference between how a deaf and hard of hearing child process information compared to a regular child?
> **Answer**: Well, yes. I would think that they would need repetition. I mean I don't understand what you are asking.

Unfortunately, two things occurred during the Impartial Hearing that I wasn't expecting. When I initially requested the Impartial Hearing I felt confident because Max's teachers had voted yes for the services so I was counting on their testimony to help Max. Unfortunately, this did not turn out to be the case. Although, Ronnie Glass spoke to Max's needs as a visual learner and how Lindamood-Bell was the "right method" she ultimately stated that SLCD was appropriate without the services. Her conclusion about SLCD didn't add up given that her entire testimony was pro Lindamood-Bell. I could only hope that the Hearing Officer, Ms. Orlando would see the inconsistencies in her testimony. Ms. Matinale did a complete turnaround on the Lindamood-Bell services. Although, she voted "yes" during the CSE Meeting her opinion changed during the Impartial Hearing. She said she only voted "yes" to the services being appropriate because they were deemed appropriate in the past.[35] The Lindamood-Bell services were never on Max's IEP so why she felt they were considered appropriate in the past as a reason to base her decision at the CSE didn't make sense to me. She claimed now that she understood about the services she no longer felt they were appropriate. She also claimed she couldn't remember what was said about Lindamood-Bell at the deposition even though it was only seventy two hours before the hearing. I didn't believe her.

My theory was that the District recommends children to SLCD providing revenue so when Marcy Laredo made her opinion about the services clear to these two teachers an unspoken understanding was established. The teachers' statements didn't just hurt my case, they solidified my belief that the system is corrupt and even teachers who initially want to help cannot hold strong under this type of pressure.

When the Impartial Hearing ended I honestly had no idea what the Hearing Officer, Ms. Orlando would decide.

---

35. Impartial Hearing testimony July 15, 2010 – P244, lines 7-19

I felt I made good points regarding the reading teacher's competency. After all, would any parent with a child who has a disability want him or her taught by these two teachers? I also felt that I proved my case against that the District and their pre-determination not to place Lindamoood-Bell on the IEP. However, Ronnie Glasses' and Ms. Matinale's statements about SLCD being appropriate without Lindamood-Bell were going to be hard for Max to overcome. While I waited for the answer, I had to send Max to SLCD, a school I had no faith in at all after Ms. Bitner's revelation and now Max's reading teachers' testimonies.

When I received Ms. Orlando's decision a few weeks later, I was devastated that she sided with the District. She didn't even address the issues of teacher competency completely disregarding it in her answer. Was it possible that an Impartial Hearing Officer could just ignore a whole portion of my argument, glossing over it like it wasn't there in black and white? I was so angry. I compiled all my information and sent it to the State Review Officer the next day.

After weeks of waiting, the State Review Officer's decided in favor of the District. Once again, my issues regarding the competency of Max's reading teachers were ignored and it was stated that the District was supplying FAPE. Was it a coincidence that both the Hearing Office and the SRO didn't address the issues of whether or not these teachers were "highly qualified?"

I had no choice but to file a New York State Complaint against SLCD for exposing my son to teachers I felt were not "Highly Qualified" to teach him. It is New York State's responsibility to make sure our teachers are trained appropriately and have more than just the base credentials to walk into a classroom. Taken directly from the New York State website: http://www.p12.nysed.gov/specialed :

The Office of Special Education works to promote educational equally and excellence for students with disabilities through its roles and responsibilities to:

- <u>oversee the implementation of Federal and State laws and policy for students with disabilities</u>;

- provide general supervision and monitoring of all public and private schools serving New York State preschool and school-age students with disabilities.

- establish a broad network of technical assistance centers and providers to work directly with parents and school districts <u>to provide current information and high quality professional development and technical assistance to improve results for students with disabilities</u>;

- ensure a system of due process, including special education mediation and impartial hearings;

- meet with stakeholders through the Commissioner's Advisory Panel for Special Education Services.

My complaint stated simply that Max's SLCD reading teachers were not trained appropriately in the reading methodologies that they were using and they did not understand the disability of deafness. I filed the complaint and learned that it was assigned to an investigator named Kathleen Kenny. Ms. Kenny had sixty days to answer my complaint. While I waited, Max was left at SLCD and there was nothing I could do about it. Every day I went to get the mail and prayed the answer would be there. As anticipated, Ms. Kenny took the entire sixty days to reply and to my utter astonishment she did not sustain the complaint. Moreover she didn't even address the points that were stated in the complaint.

1. The student's IEP does not indicate a specific reading methodology. Regulations do not require that the IEP identify the instructional methodology to be used with a student.

2. The approved private school provided the recommended program and services consistent with the IEP (i.e. special class, speech/language therapy, auditory training)

These two statements had nothing to do with the complaint. The methodologies had been established through the teachers' testimonies. Yes, SLCD provided the recommended services on the IEP but the question was whether or not they provided these services appropriately. I wasted another two months putting my faith in the state and instead I got a response from a person who skirted the issue.

I had a feeling I touched on a taboo subject that nobody wanted to address. I went all the way up the chain of command at the Special Education Quality Assurance Department and I am rebuked by all concerned. First, I called Ms. Kenny's direct supervisor Ms. Taylor who is equally talented at avoiding the issues and proceeded to argue with me. Quickly sensing she wasn't going to be of any help I continued up the chain. Next, I planned to contact Ms. Taylor's supervisor; Jacqueline Bumbalo, Up-State Region Coordinator which is a fancy title meaning she oversees the regional offices, hoping she would address my concerns regarding teacher training. I decided to write Ms. Bumbalo explaining my concerns and included my original complaint along with the response of Ms. Kenny and a description of my discussion with Ms. Taylor.

I apprehensively waited for Ms. Bumbalo's response. Keeping with the trend, Ms. Bumbalo followed the same model on how to confuse and disguise the issue. In her letter, she went as far as to say her department didn't handle these issues. Maybe Ms. Bumbalo should read her department's website.

It states on the Special Education Quality Assurance Office's website that it is responsible for monitoring special education services through a collaborative quality assurance system and providing technical assistance to schools and residents of their regions. In keeping with this role, it is indeed the responsibility of the Quality Assurance Department, to go into a school and prevent teachers from utilizing programs they were not appropriately trained in to prevent the mishandling of such programs at the hands of novice, unqualified personnel. It is indeed the responsibility of the State Quality Assurance Department to investigate the quality of teaching that is going on at SLCD, as well as the fundamentals that go into teaching these highly scientific methodologies vs. core academics. The State Quality Assurance Department cannot ignore testimony of SLCD teachers who are not able to answer basic questions regarding the disability of a child or the programs they are implementing and surmise that the law was followed solely on the degrees held by such teachers. This negates the very role of the Quality Assurance Department. The most important aspect of teaching children is the quality of teachers in the classroom so when the Quality Assurance Department washed it hands of the matter I was horrified.

I made calls to Mr. Delorenzo, State Wide Coordinator who didn't bother to return my calls. I called his supervisor Rebecca Cort, Associate Commissioner who also didn't return my calls. Continuing up the chain, I called John King, Senior Deputy Commissioner, and like the others he neglected to return my calls. No one seems to care enough to even return a phone call. Refusing to give up I sent a final packet to John King, Senior Deputy Commissioner and courtesy copied David Steiner, the Commissioner of State Education Department as well as all those involved right back to the original investigator. If nothing else, I did not want them to have deniability about the situation. Did I expect them to respond? Did I expect them to finally do their job? Did I think any of these people cared? What I received back from the state was the ultimate sidestep. And the response wasn't even from Mr. King. I guessed Mr. King was either too smart or too busy to get involved directly. Instead, he passed that responsibility down to Rebecca Cort who shut me down by writing that the investigator's decision is final and I should file for an Impartial Hearing if I didn't agree with the decision.

I came full circle. The complaint stemmed from an Impartial Hearing and their solution was another Impartial Hearing. This is truly impenetrable bureaucracy at its best. Just push it off to another department. No one is held accountable so nobody needs to care. Isn't it their job to protect the children?

When I complained to JoAnn how everyone on all levels is screwing over a little deaf boy, she always reminds me that they are screwing over all the kids, not just Max. This is a hard pill to swallow. If JoAnn's statement is true and all the kids are denied an appropriate education then something more had to be in play than just an administrative juggernaut and mean people taking advantage of it. Why are they able to get away with it? What makes this possible? There are laws in place to protect children. IDEA and *No Child Left Behind* govern special education and were designed to protect students. Was I being naïve about Congressional intent and romanticizing these laws? Now, that I was getting the run around from the State, I began to look at these laws more closely and started to wonder who these laws were really protecting.

In the end, IDEA turns out to be a fabulous scapegoat for School Districts. Congress magnanimously instituted IDEA, a law stating all disabled students deserve an education but purposefully peppered it with ambiguous wording protecting itself while seemingly taking the role of hero. Because words like "appropriate" and "reasonably calculated" are subjective words that allow Congress and the schools off the hook. Special Education children are subject to a convoluted system that graduates students unable to fill out a job application.

No Child Left Behind... a law more damaging than IDEA. For all of its bravado about setting high standards and measureable goals to improve the education outcome for children, it has failed the special education community. Sure, teachers will use scientifically researched methodologies but who is making sure they are trained properly in these methods? In my opinion, special education teachers who teach reading to disabled or special needs students using programs such as Wilson Reading Program, Orton-Gillingham and Lindamood-Bell should not be considered "highly qualified" until they meet the criteria set by those who license such programs combined with their teaching degrees and special education certificates. Congress failed these children by leaving it up to the states to decide training requirements for teachers.

Now I know why the New York State Department of Education gave me the runaround. It would be an expensive proposition if the State Quality Assurance Department found my claim that SLCD reading teachers are not trained appropriately. If word got out, other

SLCD parents would be up at arms expecting their own compensation and this would be costly. The state would never let this happen. And so the State Quality Assurance Department chooses to ignore the truth (why not, there is a loophole that allows for it) and carry on with a careless haphazard educational system because to fix it and do the job we pay them for would be the antithesis of bureaucracy.

8
My Thoughts on Advocating

"Never be afraid to raise your voice for honesty and truth and compassion against injustice and lying and greed. If people all over the world...would do this, it would change the earth."
William A. Faulkner

THE WORST PART OF THIS WHOLE EXPERIENCE for me wasn't learning about special education law or familiarizing myself with an ineffective IEP process. It wasn't all the hours I spent advocating for a service I knew belongs on Max's IEP. It wasn't Tom Korb, a man I would grow to hate. It wasn't even Max who responded with a listless, "I gotta think about this" when I excitedly told him after my third Impartial Hearing that he could go back to Lindamood-Bell. The worst part were the friendly faces who cheered me on with their encouraging words and made me feel like someone was on my side only to fold like cheap suits when it counted the most for Max. All the friendly faces and their phony Rah Rahs:

- "Don't let them bully you."

- "You need to advocate for Max; if you don't, no one will."

- "You need to fight for the services."

- "Lindamood-Bell is helping Max; he's really improved."

- "Max is lucky to have a dad like you."

School personnel who were gung-ho on the "fight" right up until the minute they attended a CSE Meeting or an Impartial Hearing. Then, I'd suddenly find myself in some twisted version of a Martin Scorsese mafia movie where my main witnesses suddenly recant their statements and can no longer remember events that took place. School personnel would back peddle, spin and finally bail on Max.

Ms. Roberts, Ronnie Glass and Ms. Matinale were just a few in a long line of educators I felt turned their backs on Max. At least I knew where the Tom Korbs of the Special Education Industry stood and I could deal with them head on. When I was faced with teachers who unexpectedly crumbled under the pressure I didn't know how to react. I truly believed that going into these Impartial Hearings these individuals would stand up for Max and was devastated when they didn't.

In the end, what did I really expect? A teacher to come forward and admit the school was not supplying an appropriate education? But wouldn't it be great! Imagine, a teacher telling everyone in the room the truth:

8: Advocating

"Sorry, I just can't help your kid. He's got me stumped."

🍎

"I've been trying to teach Max the alphabet for eighteen months now with no success, I need help."

🍎

"We need to get some extra help with this kid because we don't know what the hell we're doing."

🍎

"I've been able to help a lot of kids during the course of my teaching career but Max isn't one of them."

🍎

"All my years of teaching and I never came across anyone like your kid. If you have any ideas, please share!"

I can almost understand the teachers' behavior with the pressures placed on them by the District. But I found the behavior of the parent member who spoke so vehemently against the services perplexing. Her actions made me reflect on the role of the parent member and what could have motivated her to vote against the services. And the only explanation I could come up with that made any sense to me was she had something to gain by taking such a definitive stand. To compare a parent member who has a child currently in the system to a convict in bed with the prison guards isn't a flattering picture but it is apt. They have their own needs that need to be met so selling out another parent to get services for their own child is a survival instinct. It would seem that the powers of the School District Administrators are great and their budget minded wills massively strong trickling down corrupting all. You may read this and think; this man is a conspiracy theorist and thinks the world is against him. And I reply,

"Not the world just the North Shore School District."

I will always advocate for Max notwithstanding my experiences with the District and my feelings regarding the Special Education Industry as a whole. I see tremendous value in advocating for a child. Even when I didn't know what the hell I was doing I was able to achieve so much on Max's behalf. I would encourage all parents to be active participants at CSE meetings and don't be afraid to voice your opinion or look the fool because you may just end up with exactly what your child needs.

9
The Domino Effect

"One good parent is worth 10,000 school masters"
Chinese Proverbs

MAX IS TWELVE YEARS OLD and is still reeling from the effects of his first two years in District. Simply put, what happened to him is not an easy fix. As we age, it takes more time, effort and energy to learn things that come more easily to a younger mind. As "experienced educators," this District is obviously aware of this fact. Their refusal to recognize the damage done to Max in those first two years and their failure to rectify it, is contemptible to me. And yes, as educators, they should have been playing "catch up" instead of "hide and seek."

I fight for these services because they inflicted irreparable damage on my son and now want to skulk away. The School District not doing their job for two years; opened a Pandora's Box insidiously wrecking havoc in all areas of his young life. Imagine an eight, nine, ten year old boy attending school year round and then three days a week attending tutoring for two hours. Imagine this same boy coming home from school and tutoring only to practice what he learned from the tutoring session as well as doing his homework. Now, imagine it happening every day with no real breaks and all the while he knows other kids are running around outside, participating in sports, watching T.V., on their computers and playing video games. They are just plain having fun and he's stuck in a state of perpetual learning. Imagine missing summer vacations, trips to visit Grandparents, hanging out with friends. Max's young life has not been defined by his deafness as I initially feared but by the failures of an education system to educate.

And what about us, Max's parents? Where lays our blame in this mess? Although, I cannot speak for Patrizia, I know I have failed Max in so many ways and there are about a million things I would do differently. I played Monday morning quarterback in my head more times than I can count. If only I had done things differently, Max would not be suffering. What if I'd taken Max out of the Sea Cliff School that first year or even that second year and placed him anywhere else. I am sure every parent has had these thoughts; it can have a crippling effect. Every decision I make on behalf of Max regarding his education is an exhausting event as I weigh the pros and cons, not wanting to counter effect any progress being made. Not trusting the School District is a major obstacle in making these decisions. Because let's face it; this District has lied to me on so many occasions, it's hard to take them at face value. At this point, if Tom Korb told me the sky is blue, I am sure I would look up.

You cannot close Pandora's box once it has been opened. The focus on Max's education robbed him of any balance in his life creating more problems for the kid. Yes, Max is reading and understanding things better thanks to Lindamood-Bell. But socially, Max took a catastrophic hit. Stuck in SLCD all day with children who are bused

9: The Domino Effect

in from areas across Long Island and Queens, it doesn't make for easy friendships. Play dates are not easy when the closest kid lives an hour away. Adding to the problem, Max is two years older than most of the kids in his class. As a result Max had not been exposed to the neighborhood kids, has a hard time relating to kids his age, has no street smarts, no sense of the nuances when it comes to maneuvering on the playgrounds, and is very sensitive. This combination is not good for a budding teenager.

For a child with learning challenges, this is a nasty side effect of spending most of his life chained to a desk. Unfortunately no amount of tutoring can fix this problem. If you think getting a child to read is difficult, try getting him friends. It was easy when Max was younger and I could be his best friend, but now he is twelve years old and he wants to be part of the crowd; it's hard to explain to him why he isn't. He sees his older sister going out with friends and taking part in after-school activities. Naturally, he wants this for himself. In my defense, I was a parent with a child going into third grade who was essentially illiterate and I panicked. I had no clear answers about how to begin to teach him so the last thing on my mind was play dates. Fast forward, I now have a son with no real connection to anyone his age. Max wants to makes friends but it is under less than optimal conditions.

The first thing I thought to solve this problem was to get Max into organized sports where he would be exposed to neighborhood kids. It would be hard with his school schedule but it was necessary to build on his socialization skills. For the last few years, Max has joined soccer, baseball and basketball teams. This poor kid is running ragged between school, tutoring and sports. I volunteer to coach because I can't help myself. I want to protect him so I am having a hard time letting go. His exposure has been limited so he doesn't understand the fundamentals of the games but I am pleasantly surprised that he is a pretty good athlete. As usual, I press hard, forcing him to learn immediately what other children learn gradually through rites of passage in the school yard and on the streets. Max is apprehensive and nervous about messing up the game for his teammates; he doesn't want to be the reason for a loss. He is the odd man, he doesn't know these kids and they all know each other from school.

The kids are nice enough but the average twelve year old doesn't have the patience or understanding it takes to deal with Max. They have their established friends and it is hard for Max to break into the crowd. When he attempts to get into the mix, it is disheartening for me to watch as kids slink away from him. All it takes is one time for Max not to hear a directive during a game, or shout-out by another kid down the street and he is quickly dismissed. It's rough out there and Max has no survival instincts. He isn't confident and will back off a situation vs. a confrontation. I feel I am the only parent on the planet who wants his kid to swear and use slang because it means he is becoming one of the crowd. When another kid begins to walk away, I want him to shout, "Hey come back, I'm deaf, say it again." But it doesn't happen and Max is left wondering what he did wrong.

Sometimes, when I drive through the neighborhood on my way to wherever, I catch a glimpse of kids hanging out, riding their bikes or playing a pickup game in the park and I think how lonely Max must be at times. During these times, I find myself once again playing Monday-morning-quarterback, thinking only if Max had been introduced to the neighborhood kids at a younger age, they would have grown up together and been more accepting of the situation. Organized sports have helped but not enough. The fact is that Max needs to toughen up, be a little pushy and stand his ground with these kids. And the only way to achieve this now is to throw him to the wolves and for me to stay home.

Last year, I tried a new approach and signed Max up for the Boys and Girl Club, Locust Valley, N.Y. The program has made all the difference. He is finally coming out of his shell and making friends with the neighborhood kids. His social skills have improved greatly and he is finally grasping slang and how kids interact with each other. He no longer wants to hang with his dad. I was recently informed that I was boring and just the other day I asked him to do something and he shot back "Whatever!" I am saddened, annoyed and proud all at the same time.

The new approach is working.

Who would have thought that trying something new could change everything.

10
Where Do We Go From Here?

"Alone we can do so little; together we can do so much."
Helen Keller

LOSING THIS LAST IMPARTIAL HEARING and SRO decision was a definite blow at a crucial time in Max's education. I do not want to lose momentum when he is turning a corner on reading. Recently, I noticed Max reading these Japanese action books "Inu Yasha" that Ryan brought home. This was the first time Max was taking an initiative and reading material he picked up on his own. The content of these books was definitely more complex than the children's picture books that are scattered around his bedroom. Does he understand everything he is reading? I am not sure, but it is a start. I know that first comes interest, then later understanding and Max has an interest which is a beautiful beginning. He knows the books are a series and he needs to follow the correct storyline for it to make sense. He enthusiastically shares what he is reading.

Negative decisions of an Impartial Hearing Officer and a SRO mean very little to me. Their decisions are based on stunted information, provided by puppets, strung along by financially driven puppeteers. What do they know of the history of Max?

August 2010 Max received his second cochlear implant. We tease him about finally having surround sound but we are hoping it will make a difference in how quickly he acquires information.

Max did not attend Lindamood-Bell from October 2010 until February 2011. I cashed out what little I could in my 401K and enrolled Max in Lindamood-Bell at the beginning of 2011. I cannot afford all he needs but he will get whatever I can manage. Once again I had to make a decision affecting Max's future; I could only afford one service for him; reading or math. It was a difficult choice. I choose Math because he is only slightly behind so I figure if Lindamood-Bell can work with Max quickly to get him caught up I can switch back to reading. It's another gamble I have to take on his behalf.

When I told Max he was going back to Lindamood-Bell he was upset. He would be losing the freedom he had so easily grown accustomed to over the last few months. He reacted as any kid that doesn't want to do something and shouted, "Do I have to?" I responded, "Yes!"

I informed the School District of my actions and that I planned to seek reimbursement. During Max's CSE Meeting for his sixth grade IEP I requested Lindamood-Bell services for both reading and math and was unilaterally denied by Mr. Korb who simply stated, "I disagree with the recommendation," and further stated "I would like to thank everyone for their input, but I am the chairperson of the committee and I am going to cause the recommendation to go in a particular direction."

Epilogue

LAST YEAR MAX ATTENDED LINDAMOOD-BELL working with their program Cloud Nine for Math. Max quickly adjusted to being back at Lindamood-Bell. Max mastered decimals, fractions and word problems. I feel my gamble has paid off.

Max's fifth grade year and last at SLCD was his most productive. Max's teachers were good but I still had problems with the goals they listed on Max's IEP which I felt were dumbed down and too generic. I spent a great deal of time this year trying to get them to define the goals and challenge Max. My opinion of the reading teachers at SLCD has not wavered.

Max has reentered Mill Neck Manor for sixth grade. At the open house I was able to listen to Max's teachers talk about the curriculum and it made me feel Mill Neck was the best place for Max to go at this time. I am optimistic Mill Neck will challenge Max and I am hopeful Max will do well. My main issue is Mill Neck does not have a specified reading program. Mill Neck uses Literacy Collaborative which is basically a frame work for literacy, reading and writing. Mill Neck is using the Singapore math program which they just started using last year. Max wants to learn sign language and in support of his wish I have been taking classes so we can learn together.

I will continue to fight the North Shore School District for the Lindamood-Bell services but decided I could use a little help. I recently retained a special education attorney to aide me in my quest for Lindamood-Bell services.

My relationship with my kids is a work in progress.

Ryan and I have our have our good and bad days. She grew up while I was busy and now I have to wait to spend time with her. I am working on mending our relationship. We have coffee dates and I listen as she tells me all about the soap opera that is high school. She is a busy, beautiful girl so I wait patiently for her to call or text and tell me she has time for coffee. She recently got her driving permit and I enthusiastically volunteer driving lessons.

My relationship with Max is very much on track although there are times when I know I am pushing too hard. I am always on and I can see he finds me exhausting at times like the day we were at a driving range hitting golf balls. I could not help myself and kept giving him advice on how to hold the club, where he should stand, where he should position his feet. "Dad, just leave me alone," he complained but I would continue to push. Finally, he could take no more and whipped off his implant, positioned himself and hit the ball straight down the line.

He is learning to walk away and I am learning to let go.

Acknowledgements

MANY TEACHERS HAVE SHOWN ME there is more to learning than just academics. Coping abilities: the ability to think forward, see the bigger picture and act with kindness were paramount to their lessons and have proved invaluable in my life. What set these teachers apart from other teachers was their want and desire to help students learn. They did this because they wanted to teach, inspire and develop a love of learning. More than the subjects of the day they were interested in teaching the value of learning. Some of the many mentors in my life: James Dyne, typing teacher who gave the class the understanding that this skill would make the rest of our lives easier. I type everyday and everyday I am thankful I listened to Mr. Dyne. Lois Noon, economics teacher who would not let her students give up and refused to let us fail. Edward Koch, biology teacher: Mr. Koch made every class enjoyable by teaching through a combination of humor, fun and sharing his life experiences. Richard Langfeld, chemistry teacher: He made the world of science interesting but more importantly, understandable. Thomas Fauvell, history teacher / wrestling coach: Of all my teachers Coach Fauvell taught me one of most important lessons of all, the "WEB" of success. Want it, put forth the Effort, and Believe you can do it! I am blessed to have had these teachers in my life.

Acknowledgements

Scott Heaney, my lifelong friend who has always been there like a brother. Scott gave me the $425.00 for Max's initial consultation at Lindamood-Bell when I could not afford it. It was hard to admit I didn't have the funds to help my son but when I just started to ask, Scott said mid-sentence "Check or cash, how do you want it." I couldn't be more grateful to have a friend that was only focused on getting me what I needed. As my battle with The North Shore School District raged on Scott asked me to come work for him. It was never clear to me if the reason Scott hired me was because he needed help or he knew I needed help. As I fought the School District, Scott always made sure I was able to get off work whenever I needed. As Scott couldn't fight my fight, he always stood behind me ever pushing me forward. Scott's remarkable generosity gave my son the gift of reading.

Katharine Gibson (AKA) mom has always been there to lend a helping hand. When I had first found out that Max had a hearing issue my first call was to mom. As I started to say, "Hello" she sensed immediately something wasn't right and asked "What's wrong?" Moms always know when their children need them. As I explained that Max was not hearing she started listing off names and numbers of people I needed to call. Thanks mom for always being there. Just goes to show you that no matter how old you get, you always need your mom.

Carl Martin, Regional Director of Lindamood-Bell for taking the time to attend CSE meetings and Impartial Hearings year after year on Max's behalf. You've shown great patience and character while repeatedly being subjected to the North Shore District's attorney Gibson, as she questioned both your integrity and credentials. You are a true man of character who was able to withstand the inappropriate onslaught of character assassinations that were completely uncalled-for with grace. You and your staff did what Max's school couldn't. You taught Max to read.

Steven "Doc" Martello who always offers a constant ear and always has kind, encouraging words to offer. You are never too busy to listen and it is always with a genuine ear. In those times where I felt I couldn't take another step it was your words of wisdom that gave me the strength to push on and for that I cannot thank you enough. Thank you for your wisdom, encouraging words and most of all your friendship.

Bill Anthony Jr. You listened and understood my situation. When I needed someone to watch over my accounts you were there. You were always loyal to me and took care of my clients needs while I was off fighting for Max. In this world it is inspirational to have friends you can trust.

When I think of the people that have truly nurtured Max in his learning experiences, I will think kindly of **Lindamood-Bell, the Glen Cove Soccer League,** and **The Grenville Bakers Boy and Girls Club of Locust Valley.** Each has contributed in their own unique wonderful way to Max's journey to becoming a happy successful young man.

I want to express my deepest and dearest thanks to **JoAnn Higgins**. Two years into the battle with the North Shore School District JoAnn walked into my life. From the moment we met JoAnn became my sounding board. Before JoAnn got the chance to meet Max, she was inundated with all the issues I was having with the North Shore School District about a boy she didn't know. She learned firsthand what I was going through and constantly looked and found ways to assist me in my quest to aid Max. At every turn JoAnn was there with encouragement, advice and support to help ensure success for Max. Never, did I realize that when we met; JoAnn would inspire me in so many ways. Through JoAnn I have learned patience and understanding which have helped me to be a better dad. JoAnn is always standing on the sideline helping me to build the best relationship I can with my children. Many a time JoAnn has surprised me with events that will ensure I have time with Ryan and Max. Without JoAnn this book would never have been read. She first inspired me to write Max's story and then spent countless hours turning my dissertation into something readable. JoAnn's insight and constant pulling me back and not allowing me to be a hover dad showed me that Max was able to succeed on his own. JoAnn continues to teach me so many things one of which "is to let go." Every day I am thankful you walked into my life. You are to me what one could only dream to have yet I have you my dream.

Appendix

SRO Decision: Excerpt (4/22/09)

Ronni Glass: Letter recommending LMB (5/15/09)

Tom Korb: Letter stating District will comply with SRO (6/9/2009)

Finding from NYS Department of Education: Excerpt (7/21/2009)

Jacqueline Bumbalo, Up State Coordinator: Letter (4/12/2011)

Rebecca Cort, Associate Commissioner: Letter (5/13/2011)

Appendix: SRO Decision: Excerpt (4/22/09)

Application of a Child with a Disability, Appeal No. 05-041; Application of a Child with a Disability, Appeal No. 04-054; Application of the Bd. of Educ., Appeal No. 02-047).

The New York State Legislature amended the Education Law to place the burden of production and persuasion upon the school district during an impartial hearing, except that a parent seeking tuition reimbursement for a unilateral placement has the burden of production and persuasion regarding the appropriateness of such placement (Educ. Law § 4404[1][c], as amended by Ch. 583 of the Laws of 2007). The amended statute took effect for impartial hearings commenced on or after October 14, 2007; therefore, it applies to the instant case (see Application of the Bd. of Educ., Appeal No. 08-016).

The parent argues on appeal that the student requires additional hours of Lindamood-Bell reading services after school each day in order for him to receive appropriate educational benefits. As discussed above, the student exhibits a language-based learning disability and significantly delayed receptive language skills, which may in part be a result of his hearing loss (Dist. Exs. 7 at p. 7; 8 at p. 4). The student's extremely low range of cognitive functioning also negatively affects his ability to learn (Dist. Ex. 7 at p. 3). After a series of meetings, the CSE recommended that the student be placed at SLCD in a 12:2+2 special class program that focused on the relationship between language development and academic success (Dist. Exs. 6 at p. 1; 15 at p. 1). The hearing record describes SLCD as employing a transdisciplinary program model that utilizes a professional team of educators and therapists to coordinate each student's instructional goals and activities (Dist. Ex. 15 at p. 1). The school evaluates each student to identify appropriate reading programs that emphasize phonemic awareness and semantic language development based on the student's identified needs (id.). The school offers differentiated levels of group instruction and 90 minutes of "intensive" daily reading instruction using the Milestones, Recipe for Reading, Wilson, Edmark, and Fast ForWord programs (id.). The hearing record also reflects that classrooms at SLCD are equipped with "FM sound field systems" to optimize teacher-student voice quality and increase students' listening skills (id. at p. 2). The September 4, 2008 CSE meeting minutes revealed that the CSE determined that the parent's requested Lindamood-Bell services were unnecessary based on the SLCD representatives' description of "the extent" of their reading program, which the CSE believed would benefit the student (Dist. Ex. 6 at p. 5). The September 4, 2008 IEP also reflected that the CSE modified the student's annual goals based on the results of August 2008 assessments conducted by Lindamood-Bell (id.).

The hearing record reveals that the CSE's recommended program and services as stated on the student's September 4, 2008 IEP reflected the student's present levels of performance, and the information provided by the student's 2008 neuropsychological evaluation and his January 2008 speech-language evaluation (compare Dist. Ex. 6, with Dist. Exs. 7; 8; 15). I find that the recommended program as envisioned by the September 4, 2008 CSE was reasonably calculated to provide educational benefits to the student during the 2008-09 school year, reflected the requisite alignment between the student's special education needs and his goals necessary for the provision of an appropriate program in the LRE, and provided for the student to be grouped with students of similar special education needs and abilities. Regarding the reading program offered at SLCD, the hearing record reflects that SLCD evaluates students to identify an appropriate reading program for each student which emphasizes phonemic awareness and semantic language

Appendix: SRO Decision: Excerpt (4/22/09)

development (Dist. Ex. 15 at p. 1). With regard to this student's reading program, the district's director of special education testified that in addition to English language arts, SLCD provides daily, half-hour sessions each of the Milestones program, the Recipe for Reading program and the Fast ForWord program (Tr. pp. 91-92). The Milestones reading program is described by the student's teacher at SLCD as addressing sight word vocabulary, comprehension, processing, spelling, fluency, and sequencing (Tr. pp. 324, 325). She testified that students are pretested to determine their instructional level in the program, and then put into groups and that the student was in a group of either two or three children (Tr. p. 327). The Recipe for Reading program was described by the student's SLCD teacher as "a multisensory, visual, auditory, kinesthetic approach to phonetics and phonics, based on an Orton-Gillingham methodology" (Tr. pp. 329-30). The student's SLCD teacher described the Fast ForWord program as an individualized computer program that addresses auditory comprehension wherein the student progresses from one level to the next based on his correct responses (Tr. p. 331). The student's teacher at SLCD testified, without further explanation or referencing any objective evidence, that the student is "progressing" in the Milestones and Recipe for Reading programs (Tr. pp. 327-328, 330, 331). However, the extent of the student's progress in these programs is not further elucidated nor is the brief statement about progress referenced to the student's IEP goals.

Although I have determined that the program as formulated by the CSE was reasonably calculated to confer educational benefits to the student at the time it was designed, the hearing record does not demonstrate that the student's program provided at SLCD was being provided in conformity with the student's September 4, 2008 IEP. The term "free appropriate public education" means special education and related services that-- (A) have been provided at public expense, under public supervision and direction, and without charge; (B) meet the standards of the State educational agency; (C) include an appropriate preschool, elementary school, or secondary school education in the State involved; and (D) *are provided in conformity with the individualized education program* required under section 1414(d) of this title (20 U.S.C. § 1401[9]) (emphasis added). In this case, the hearing record does not show that the student's otherwise appropriate IEP was properly implemented (8 NYCRR 200.4[e][7]; Application of a Child with a Disability, Appeal No. 08-087). The student's SLCD teacher testified that as of October 28, 2008 she had only reviewed the testing accommodations portion of the student's IEP (Tr. pp. 309-10, 349-50, 369-73). The teacher's testimony revealed that she was providing instruction without utilizing the student's IEP. The hearing record shows that the district was not providing special education and related services in conformity with the student's IEP.

Therefore, under the circumstances of this case, the district has not met its burden to show that a FAPE was offered (see 8 NYCRR 200.4[e][3][i], [iii]). As a result, I will award additional services to the student as compensation for the deprivation of a FAPE from September 2, 2008 to at least October 28, 2008, the time period in which the student's special education teacher testified that she provided instruction without utilizing the student' IEP, but for identifying the student's test accommodation needs. I will order the district to convene a CSE meeting and develop a program to provide the student with an additional 10 hours per week of services consisting of 1:1 reading instruction, beyond his current program, utilizing a multisensory sequential approach that is individually prescriptive to meet the student's identified deficits and allows him to progress at his own pace for the remainder of the 2008-09 school year and for summer 2009. The hearing record does not show that such additional services must be

Appendix: SRO Decision: Excerpt (4/22/09)

provided through Lindamood-Bell in order for the student to receive educational benefits. I will also order the CSE, upon reconvening, to review the current implementation of the student's IEP. Therefore, I will modify the impartial hearing officer's order to be consistent with this decision.

I have considered the parties' remaining contentions and need not reach them in light of my determination herein. Lastly, unless the parties otherwise agree, the additional services ordered herein are to end at the conclusion of their provision during summer 2009 as ordered and are not to serve as a basis for any future pendency services.

THE APPEAL IS SUSTAINED TO THE EXTENT INDICATED.

IT IS ORDERED that the impartial hearing officer's decision is hereby annulled to the extent that it determined that the student was being provided with a FAPE for the 2008-09 school year; and

IT IS FURTHER ORDERED, unless the parties otherwise agree, that the district reconvene a CSE within 15 calendar days of the receipt of this decision to revise the student's 2008-09 IEP to include 1:1 reading instruction, beyond his current program, utilizing a multisensory sequential approach that is individually prescriptive to meet the student's identified deficits and allows him to progress at his own pace for 10 hours per week for the remainder of the 2008-09 school year as additional compensatory services; and

IT IS FURTHER ORDERED, unless the parties otherwise agree, that 1:1 reading instruction utilizing a multisensory sequential approach that is individually prescriptive to meet the student's identified deficits and allows for him to progress at his own pace be offered to the student as additional compensatory services for 10 hours per week, for six weeks during summer 2009; and

IT IS FURTHER ORDERED, unless the parties otherwise agree, that such additional reading services for the remainder of the 2008-09 school year shall be implemented no later than 30 calendar days after the date of this decision; and

IT IS FURTHER ORDERED, that upon reconvening, the CSE shall review the current implementation of the student's IEP.

Dated: Albany, New York
April 22, 2009

PAUL F. KELLY
STATE REVIEW OFFICER

Appendix: Ronni Glass: Letter recommending LMB (5/15/09)

5/15/09

I have been asked my opinion of as to whether the Wilson Reading program vs the Lindamood Bell Visualizing and Verbalizing program would best benefit Max at this time. Although I am not trained specifically as a reading teacher, from my knowledge and training as a speech pathologist/audiologist and research, I have concluded that the Wilson Reading Program is mainly for improving reading decoding and spelling. When decoding improves, it stands to reason that an improvement in comprehension will also take place. While this is also true of the Lindamood LIPS Program, their other programs "Seeing Stars" (the one Max was on this past summer), goes a step further and the "Visualizing and Verbalizing Program" is specifically designed for better understanding and memory of language, reading comprehension and oral language expression. These are the very areas where Max has weaknesses. The Wilson Program consists of 12 steps that is direct, sequential and multisensory (visual, auditory, tactile), but can be modified by the instructors to fit into the school's scheduling (spread out over time) It is successful since students only read text that has been previously taught. It is described as a "philosophy" of reading instruction. Whereas the Lindamood Bell program has a specific multisensory (visual, auditory, tactile and oral motor) concentrated approach (often administered by more than one individual) which seems to lead to its success. Although the Lindamood program can also be modified and its approach utilized, it is not recommended by Lindamood Bell to do so. The Visualizing and Verbalizing Program is specifically designed to strengthen the student's concept imagery, rather than only reading what has already been taught. Students are more apt to be able to transfer these skills to academic studies. It also helps to develop note taking ability, attention skills, memory, ability to recall facts, get the main idea, infer, conclude, predict and evaluate. It supposedly helps to improve critical thinking skills by integrating imagery and language. In other words, the Lindamood Bell programs go beyond teaching decoding and spelling.

Max has had the Wilson Reading Program at Northshore prior to attending Linadamood Bell and SLCD, and had little success. His decoding skills were significantly impaired prior to last summer. He had the Lindamood program for the summer last year and met with excellent success and significant improvement in his decoding ability. He has retained what he has learned and continued to improve in his decoding skills with the Recipe for Reading, Fast ForWord and individual therapy programs at SLCD. His decoding skills are significantly better, but continued strengthening for fluency is needed. Since, he did not meet with success when on the Wilson Reading Program, it seems counter productive to return to this program. I have always been taught that when one program used consistently does not seem to work, it is time to change programs. Since the Lindamood Bell program was successful and the next program (Visualizing and Verbalizing) is specifically designed to address comprehension (language and reading), it seems obvious to use the Visualizing and Verbalizing (Lindamood Bell) program for remediation of his language and reading

Appendix: Ronni Glass: Letter recommending LMB (5/15/09)

comprehension. This concentrated program administered by trained professionals is the recommended version that Max has met with success in the past and is most likely to meet with continued success.

Ronni Glass, Au.D., CCC/SLP/A

Incl: Descriptions of Wilson and Lindamood Bell Programs

North Shore
Central School District
280 Carpenter Avenue • Sea Cliff, New York 11579
(516) 277-7900 • Fax (516) 277-7905

Thomas A. Korb
Director of Special Education

June 9, 2009

Thomas W. Gibson
6 Harbor Hill Road
Glen Cove, New York 11542

RE: Maximilian Gibson

Dear Mr. Gibson:

This letter asserts that North Shore Central School District will comply with the State Review Officer's 4/22/09 order by utilizing the services of Lindamood-Bell (Roslyn). Services will be provided two hours daily beginning 5/4/09 through the last day of the 2008—2009 school year. Since the service will start subsequent to 5/4/09, the District agrees make up services missed between 5/4/09 and the actual start date of the Lindamood-Bell service. Moreover, the services ordered for the summer of 2009 will also be provided by utilizing the services of Lindamood-Bell.

Yours truly,

Thomas A. Korb
Director of Special Education

Appendix: Finding from NYS Department of Education: Excerpt (7/21/2009)

student's special education program, and make recommendations for the 2009-10 school year. In attendance at the meeting were the following staff from the North Shore School District:

T. Korb, Director of Special Education and Chairperson
W. Kitay, Psychologist
M. Schleifman, Regular Education Teacher
K. Demeo, Speech-Language Therapist
R. Cooper, Occupational Therapist

Also, participating by teleconference, were the following staff from SLCD:

A. Lee, Psychologist
H. Lockel, Special Education Teacher
T. Bitner, Special Education Teacher
R. Glass, Speech-Language Therapist

D. Blancharski, Parent Member, T. Gibson, Parent, and R. Miller, Friend of Parent also attended.

The recommendations from the May 4, 2009 CSE meeting included reading instruction 1:1, once daily for 2 hours for the remainder of the 2008-09 school year, and reading instruction 1:1, once daily, for 2 hours for the Extended School Year, summer, 2009.

In a letter, dated May 8, 2009, from Mr. Korb to the parent, reading instruction, which was to begin on May 18, 2009, would be provided by Ms. Carol Speranza, special education teacher employed by the District.

On June 9, 2009, in a letter from Mr. Korb to the parent, the District stated, "This letter asserts that the North Shore Central School District will comply with the State Review Officer's 4/22/09 order by utilizing the services of Lindamood-Bell (Roslyn). Services will be provided two hours daily beginning 5/4/09 through the last day of the 2008-2009 school year. Since the service will start subsequent to 5/4/09, the District agrees to make up services missed between 5/4/09 and the actual start date of the Lindamood-Bell service. Moreover, the services ordered for the summer of 2009 will also be provided by utilizing the services of Lindamood-Bell."

Conclusions:
The parent reported that he wanted the Lindamood-Bell method used in the reading instruction for the student provided by an outside agency. The parent claimed that the student had success when he was instructed by an outside agency using the Lindamood-Bell method during the summer of 2008. The parent alleged that the Wilson method was not "multi-sensory" as ordered by the SRO and did not meet the needs of the student, whereas the Lindamood-Bell method did fulfill the requirements of the order. Regulations do not require that the CSE recommend and include on the IEP the specific methodology to be used to instruct the student or the individual that will provide

the service. However, when a parent exercises their due process rights and challenges the recommendations of the CSE, a school district is required to comply with the decision and order of the Impartial Hearing Officer/State Review Officer. Therefore, the CSE was required to recommend/provide reading instruction that utilizes a "multisensory sequential approach that is individually prescriptive to meet the student's identified deficits and allows him to progress at his own pace."

To determine the appropriate services to meet the individual needs of a student, a school district, whenever the CSE reviews a student's program, will consider [8NYCRR 200.4(f)]:

- The strengths of the student
- The concerns of the parent for enhancing the education of the child
- The results of the most recent evaluation of the student

Although the District changed its initial decision, and recommended methodology and staffing that the parent believed were appropriate, the parent did not want to withdraw the complaint because he believed that Mr. Korb, the Chairperson of the May 4, 2009 CSE meeting did not comply with the SRO order since he did not allow the CSE to function as a commitee. The parent claims that the meeting was not conducted according to regulation. The parent stated in his written complaint, "CSE is to be a committee. Mr. Korb did not allow the CSE to run as a committee by being the sole decision maker. It is Mr. Korb's responsibility as the chairperson to get the input from all the members of the committee. Mr. Korb never asked or allowed the committee to give input on what would be an appropriate approach for Maximilian to receive the ordered services." Federal Regulation 300.23 states that an Individualized Education Program Team or IEP Team means a group of individuals that is responsible for developing, reviewing, or revising an IEP for a child with a disability. Guidance from the United States Department of Education indicates that decisions made at CSE meetings are to be made based upon informed participation of all members and consensus agreement to the recommendations. However, "the IEP Team should work toward consensus, but the public agency has ultimate responsibility to ensure that the IEP includes the services that the child needs in order to receive free appropriate public education (FAPE). It is not appropriate to make IEP decisions based upon a majority vote" (34 CFR 300, Question 9). Therefore, when the CSE does not reach consensus, the chairperson as representative of the school district must make the recommendations. However, this does not negate the chairperson's responsibility to ensure all members have an opportunity to participate and consider the concerns of the parent and that the parent be provided with Prior Written Notice (PWN) that meets regulatory requirements. Whenever a district proposes to or refuses to initiate or change the identification, evaluation, educational placement of the student or the provision of FAPE, the parent must receive a written notice that includes a description of the action proposed or refused by the district and an explanation of why the district proposes or refuses to take the action.

Appendix: Finding from NYS Department of Education: Excerpt (7/21/2009)

The parent provided the State Education Department (SED) with a CD recording of the May 4, 2009 CSE meeting. In the segment of the meeting that addressed the SRO order, there was no discussion of the reading instruction. The chairperson, Mr. Korb stated that the District would comply with the order by providing the SRO mandated reading instruction. However, when the parent attempted to discuss methodology, Mr. Korb stated that the methodology and location of the service would be decided after the meeting. Although there is no requirement that the CSE determine methodology and include a specific methodology on an IEP, regulation does require that the concerns of the parent for enhancing the education of the child be considered as stated in 8NYCRR 200.4(f). The Prior Written Notice (PWN) for the 2008-2009 IEP also does not reflect that the CSE considered the parent's concerns. In addition, the revised IEP for the 2008-2009 school year and the 2009-2010 school year for Extended School Year services do not reflect the SRO order that the IEP include reading instruction that is multisensory.

Based on a review of information/documentation as described above, the allegation is sustained.

Allegation 1 Status: Sustained

Compliance Assurance Plan

Allegation # 1   **Citation # 200.5(k)(3)**   **Due Date: 08/21/2009**

Required Corrective Action
1. The District will amend the student's 2008-2009 IEP and the 2009-2010 IEP for Extended School Year to state that reading instruction is provided using a multisensory approach, and provide a copy of the IEPs to all who are responsible for IEP implementation.
2. The District will issue Prior Written Notices to the parent that include statements of what the CSE considered at the May 4, 2009 CSE meeting, and what the CSE proposed to provide and what the CSE refused to provide.
3. The District will provide the reading instruction as ordered by the SRO.

Evidence to Verify Compliance
1. The District will provide SED with copies of the amended IEPs. The District will submit evidence that copies of the amended IEPs have been provided to all who are responsible for IEP implementation.
2. The District will provide SED with copies of the PWNs. The District will submit evidence that the parent has been provided with the PWNs.
3. The District will provide SED with evidence that the reading instruction has been

Appendix: Jacqueline Bumbalo, Up State Coordinator: Letter (4/12/2011)

THE STATE EDUCATION DEPARTMENT / THE UNIVERSITY OF THE STATE OF NEW YORK / ALBANY, NY 12234

OFFICE OF P-12 EDUCATION: Office of Special Education
UPSTATE SPECIAL EDUCATION QUALITY ASSURANCE
State Tower Building, 109 S. Warren Street, Suite 320 • Syracuse, NY 13202
www.p12.nysed.gov/speciated

Phone: (315) 476-5645
Fax: (315) 476-5182

April 12, 2011

Mr. Thomas Gibson
6 Harbor Hill Road
Glen Cove, NY 11542

Dear Mr. Gibson:

In response to your request, I have reviewed the findings of the State complaint you initiated on December 1, 2010 and the issues you raised in your letter to the New York State Education Department (NYSED) dated March 30, 2011. You reported in your letter that the findings of the investigation failed to address two legal issues set forth in your State complaint, namely, that the approved private school serving your son, Max Gibson, failed to:

- appropriately train teachers in scientifically based reading methodologies in accordance with No Child Left Behind (NCLB) and,
- properly implement your son's Individualized Education Program (IEP) in accordance with the Individuals with Disabilities Education Act (IDEA) because teachers were never appropriately trained in the scientifically based reading methodologies they were utilizing.

Let me first address your concern that the teachers at the approved private school your son attended failed to appropriately train your son's teachers in scientifically based reading methodologies. State regulations authorize the NYSED to investigate allegations of a violation of the Part 300 of the Code of Federal Regulations and Part 200 of the Regulations of the Commissioner of Education relating to the education of students with disabilities. The reason that the NYSED did not address the allegation regarding teacher training in the State complaint is because the NYSED is limited to making a determination if a teacher is appropriately certified pursuant to Part 80 of the Regulations of the Commissioner (8NYCRR 200.6 (b) (4) but **not** to assess if that teacher has been appropriately trained in a particular methodology. Although you present information in correspondence to the Department establishing what you believe are weaknesses in the preparation of the teachers serving your son, the formal State complaint process is not the appropriate means of addressing your first concern.

Your second allegation, regarding the improper implementation of your son's IEP, was investigated and addressed in the findings of the State complaint. The complaint investigator reviewed your son's IEP and other documentation/conducted interviews and determined that your son's IEP was implemented as it was written. The information in the findings describes the extent of the implementation. Therefore, the investigator found no violation of Part 300 of the Code of Federal Regulations and/or Part 200 of the Regulations of the Commissioner of Education related to the implementation of your child's IEP occurred.

Appendix: Jacqueline Bumbalo, Up State Coordinator: Letter (4/12/2011)

In summary, the IEP did not, nor is it required to, identify a specific reading methodology. Furthermore certified special education teachers are not required by law and regulation to have training in the Wilson reading method by a Wilson trainer in order to provide specially designed reading instruction to students with disabilities. The investigator determined that the student received the recommended special education program and services and the annual goals on the IEP were implemented by special education teachers and related service providers at the approved private school.

The findings of a State complaint are final. NYSED will, however, correct any errors that have been made with respect to the statements of fact presented in the findings. This does not appear to be the case as described in your letter.

However, when a State complaint involves the rights of an individual student, upon receipt of an adverse decision rendered in a State complaint, as in your case, you may initiate an impartial hearing to address the issues raised in the State complaint, provided that the subject of the complaint involves an issue about which a due process hearing can be filed and the two year statute of limitations for due process hearings has not expired.

Information about NYSED complaint procedures can be found at http://www.p12.nysed.gov/specialed/quality/complaintqa.htm. The investigation and findings of your State complaint were completed consistent with these procedures.

Sincerely,

Jacqueline Bumbalo
Upstate Regional Coordinator

C: Eileen Taylor
Kathleen Kenney

Appendix: Rebecca Cort, Associate Commissioner: Letter (5/13/2011)

THE STATE EDUCATION DEPARTMENT / THE UNIVERSITY OF THE STATE OF NEW YORK / ALBANY, NY 12234

ASSOCIATE COMMISSIONER, OFFICE OF P-12 EDUCATION: Office of Special Education
Tel. (518) 473-4818 Albany
     (718) 722-4558 New York City
Fax (518) 402-3534 Albany
     (718) 722-4793 New York City

May 13, 2011

Mr. Thomas Gibson
6 Harbor Hill Rd
Glen Cove, NY 11542

Dear Mr. Gibson:

Your letter to Senior Deputy Commissioner John King dated May 2, 2011 was forwarded to the Office of Special Education to inform you of the New York State Education Department's (NYSED) position regarding the findings of a State complaint.

NYSED's decision regarding a State complaint is final and cannot be appealed. NYSED has reviewed the information contained in your letter of May 2, 2011 and has not found errors that have been made with respect to facts presented in the written final decision. Disagreement with NYSED's written final decision in and of itself does not constitute a factual error.

Where a complaint involves the rights of an individual student under Article 89 of Education Law, upon receipt of an adverse decision rendered pursuant to a State complaint, the complainant or school district may initiate an impartial hearing to address issues raised in the complaint. Information regarding State complaint procedures can be found at www.p12.nysed.gov/specialed/quality/complaintqa.htm.

Sincerely,

Rebecca H. Cort

c: John B. King, Jr.
   James DeLorenzo
   Jacqueline Bumbalo
   Eileen Taylor

Glossary of Terms

Free Appropriate Public Education (FAPE)
Children with disabilities are entitled to a public education appropriate to their needs, at no cost to their families.

Committee on Special Education (CSE)
Parents are vital members of a team called the Committee on Special Education (CSE) or Committee on Preschool Special Education (CPSE) that is responsible for developing an appropriate educational program for your child. You must be given opportunities to participate in the discussion and decision-making process about your child's needs for special education.

Individual Education Plan (IEP)
An IEP is designed to meet the unique educational needs of one child, who may have a disability, as defined by federal regulations. The IEP is intended to help children reach educational goals more easily than they otherwise would. 34 CFR 300.320 In all cases the IEP must be tailored to the individual student's needs as identified by the IEP evaluation process, and must especially help teachers and related service providers (such as paraprofessional educators) understand the student's disability

and how the disability affects the learning process.

Impartial Hearing (IH) (AKA Due Process)
Parents and or a school district who are in disagreement can request a due process hearing. Here, you and the school district present written evidence about the disputed issue and have witnesses testify before a hearing officer. If you do not agree with the outcome of the hearing, you can appeal the decision all the way to state or federal court.

Impartial Hearing Officer (IHO)
Oversees an Impartial Hearing in the same way a judge oversees a court case

State Review Officer (SRO)
If a party wants to appeal an IHO's decision it is sent to the SRO who will review the case and render a decision. The SRO can either sustain the IHO's decision or over turn the decision and order remedies to either party.

State Complaint
Parents have the right to submit a written complaint to the New York State Education Department if they believe that the school district has violated a requirement under State or federal special education laws and regulations.

Individuals Disability Education Act (IDEA)
Is a federal law binding in all states. State law can mandate more protection than IDEA but not less. Each state uses different criteria to determine programs offered and guidelines for qualifying students for special education.

No Child Left Behind (NCLB)
The focus is on accountability and requires that the academic performance of all school children, including those with disabilities achieve 100% proficiency in reading and math by the year 2012.